A Ha'penny over the High Level

Acknowledgements
Tyne Bridge Publishing thank David Brown for sending us the manuscript of *A Ha'penny over the High Level*, and Tony Kenyon for his evocative illustrations.

Thanks also to George Ray Dobson who typed the manuscript from the original.

Front cover: Trams near the High Level Bridge, 1924 *(Newcastle Libraries)*

ISBN: 978 185795 118 9

Published by City of Newcastle upon Tyne
Newcastle Libraries & Information Service,
Tyne Bridge Publishing, 2007

www.tynebridgepublishing.co.uk

Printed by Athenaeum Press, Gateshead

A Ha'penny over the High Level

A Tyneside and Northumberland Childhood

Thomas Knowles Bell

Illustrated by Tony Kenyon

Tyne Bridge Publishing

Foreword

Tom Knowles Bell, always known as Knowles to his family, was my first cousin once removed – his grandfather being my great grandfather.

He put this poignant and evocative manuscript into my hands shortly before his death in 1984, and I promised to try to find a publisher. He had intended to write a second part but died before he got around to it. My promise gave him great satisfaction but left me with a nagging conscience which Tyne Bridge Publishing have now silenced – for which I thank them.

The Bell family was forced into exile from Tyneside to the dales of west Northumberland by their extreme poverty and their mother's illness. Once there, however, they were enfolded in a community whose outstanding social cohesion and altruism succoured and supported them in the enduring, if diluted, tradition of North East England.

David Brown, 2007

The Good Fight

My mother, Ada Newton, was a Cinderella without a Prince Charming. She was imposed upon when young, not by two ugly sisters and a stepmother, but by three rather good-looking cousins – Dorothy, Arthur and Knowles Frank – and by their stepmother, a snobbish, domineering woman with a heart of flint.

Ada was born in Westgate Road, Newcastle upon Tyne. Her father, Tom Newton, who worked at Clarke Chapman's as a fitter, belonged originally to Sunderland, as did the girl he married, Jane Leck Booth.

When Ada was four her mother died and her father's sister, Lizzie, and her husband George Frank, took her into their care

while the two boys, Andy and Tom, stayed with their father. There had been another girl, Bessie, in the family, but she had died from meningitis caused by a blow to the head while playing twirly swings round a lamppost.

Aunt Lizzie died quite young, while Ada was still a schoolgirl, and George Frank married again. The second Mrs Frank, whom Ada always referred to as Aunt Annie, regarded Ada as a poor relation to be tolerated rather than loved.

Agnes, the maid of all work employed by the Franks, became pregnant and, like the upright citizens they were, her employers kicked her out. Cheap labour was abundant during 'La Belle Epoch', but why spend a few pounds per year and feed the drudge when a substitute was available for nothing? Aunt Annie withdrew Ada from school to 'help with household duties'. This involved all the work previously performed by the unfortunate Agnes, including carrying scuttles of coal up several flights of stairs to all the bedrooms. There were no parties, dances, theatres or outings for Ada; her duty was to attend to the comfort of others while her cousins enjoyed a hectic social life. She was, however, allowed to attend the Wesleyan Chapel in the hopes of a better life to come.

There are photographs of the three Frank cousins holding tennis racquets or playing a violin or a mandolin beside potted palms. There are no pictures of Ada carrying scuttles of coal, scrubbing floors or laying bedroom fires.

A visiting choir from Newcastle came to the Wesleyan Chapel on West Street to perform the oratorio *Elijah*. One of the singers was destined to become my father. Somehow Ada evaded the vigilant eyes of Aunt Annie and became acquainted with Thomas Bell. Ada's nickname for him was Elijah. She was now twenty-three and, soon after their meeting and a very brief courtship, she decided to marry him.

The Franks were horrified at the thought of losing their unpaid skivvy and shocked that she would consider marrying a suitor not of their choosing. They attempted to change her mind by pointing out that her intended husband was poor, had no social position, no house and little prospect of bettering himself. They may have been right for the wrong reasons, but Ada insisted on her independence. She was married in the Wesleyan Chapel in Gateshead on New Year's Day 1914. None of the Franks attended the ceremony.

The newly married couple had neither house nor furniture and had to begin their married life in furnished rooms in Jefferson Street, Newcastle. Later that year they rented a house with a garden and a little plot of land where they could keep hens. It was in Forest Hall, which at that time was a country village with a railway station. They were very poor and had to exchange eggs for bread in a local shop. This house in the country was a dream that quickly evaporated. They could not afford the rent, so they moved to Windsor Avenue in Gateshead where I was born almost exactly one year after the wedding.

Shortly after I was born, Ada and Thomas (Mother and Father to me) moved to Bensham Road. Father became a Plymouth Brother and Mother fell among zealots so there were no more oratorios, no Elijahs or Messiahs at Christmas. Mother was a very sincere Christian throughout her life, but she deplored the austere and joyless creed of the Brethren. In spite of this she did make friends with a few of them; a Scots family who had a herbalist's shop in Gateshead were her friends for life. They visited us when we eventually moved to Swinhope and were very kind, sending her herbs for her cough. Mother had great faith in the herbs; they produced a liquid which had the most abominable taste and smell, but Mother was certain they did her good. I, too, was extremely fond of this family, but for the most part I avoided the Brethren as much as I could.

I cannot call to mind a single display of affection between my mother and father, nor can I recollect any rifts between them so they must have been moderately happy together. I think Mother's main reason for marrying was a desire to escape the Frank family. Father also seemed anxious to leave home, perhaps because he was so different from his brother, Willie, who had been right through the war and was at the Battle of the Somme. Willie also enjoyed a drink and a bit of fun and this may have produced tension at home.

My father's father had a whitesmith's forge and workshop in Pilgrim Street. I enjoyed my visits there. Grandfather Bell had a dingy little room he called the office. It contained a high desk with dusty bills and invoices impaled upon a long wire hanging on its edge. On the wall was the new-fangled contraption Grandfather hated so much – the telephone. Once I heard him having a fierce argument over the phone. Exasperated, he put back the receiver and walked away. Then thinking of something else to say he rushed back, picked it up again and began shouting, 'Hoi hoi, come back!' Uncle Willie said, 'It is no use Father, you've cut him off.' Grandfather jammed back the receiver and shouted, 'Blasted contraption!' at the instrument.

Much as he disliked the telephone, these feelings were mild compared to his attitude towards welding. He loathed the very word and would not listen when his sons pleaded with him to install welding gear and keep up with the times. Welding had taken away a large proportion of his livelihood and deprived him of the satisfaction he found in the expression of his craft. With hot iron, a hammer and an anvil Grandfather became an artist.

As a boy I used to watch him, fascinated. A couple of resonant taps on the anvil, then bang, bang, bang on the iron and it began to take on the shape of a leaf, a scroll or a curlicue; back into the forge for reheating and the process repeated until the metal

assumed its final form. The iron in his left
hand seemed to revolve of its own
accord. Finally he would finish off the
shape with some gentle taps and
place it in the cooling trough, just a
little sizzling dip at first to
get the tempering colour
right, then the final plunge
and steam would fill the
workshop.

I took great delight in
working the bellows to bring
up the heat of the fire. I would fling on
handfuls of iron, brass and copper filings
from the floor in order to watch the multi-coloured sparks leaping
up the chimney. I was, as Grandfather often said, an infernal
nuisance. Sometimes, to get rid of me, he sent me on an errand to
the ironmonger's further down the street to buy a warding file or a
drill. More rarely he gave me a penny to buy sweets. I knew in my
heart, as children do, that there was more real affection in
Grandfather's oaths than in the pious pronouncements of the
Brethren.

Before my father's death my mother took me on a visit to my
paternal grandmother's house in Lovaine Place, Newcastle, at that
time a high-class residential neighbourhood. They sent me out to
play while they had a chat. A house opposite had a pair of stone
couchant lions flanking the steps leading to the front door. They
seemed to be staring at the stone houses with their imposing
doorways and highly polished brass doorknockers, and the maids
with starched aprons and caps opening the door to callers. I sat
astride the back of one of the life-sized lions and imagined I was
riding it, but a maid came out and shooed me away. I next walked

a little way to admire a bright red three-wheeler car parked further down the road and then being bored, as there was nothing more to look at, went back to the house.

Grandmother Bell did not dislike my mother but I think she rather despised her; failing, I think, to recognize her quiet courage and unquenchable spirit. Yet their backgrounds were similar. According to Bell family legend, Grandmother had been kicked out at the age of twelve by a stepmother to fend for herself. This is probably an exaggeration, but she had gone into service at a very early age. What she achieved before marrying Grandfather is a mystery and there are, as I discovered, several different accounts. What is certain is that somehow she acquired the speech, bearing and manner of a middle-class lady. She had a very refined appearance, wore a veil over her face and carried a tightly rolled umbrella. She used this weapon occasionally to poke railway porters or shop assistants in the back to attract their attention. Once, to my great astonishment, she poked a policeman, who, when he turned round, touched his helmet in salute and addressed her as 'Ma'am'.

One incident stays in my mind as clearly as if it had happened yesterday: My grandmother and I were walking down Northumberland Street when she decided to board a tram. Just as we approached, the conductor rang the bell and the tram moved off and gathered speed. Grandmother hooked her umbrella on a rail at the rear of the tram and began running behind, still holding my hand. It must have been a strange sight to passers-by – an old lady and a child sprinting behind a tram, hooked on to it with an umbrella. Luckily the conductor saw us and gave the emergency stop signal. The tram stopped and we got on. She flung back her veil and berated the conductor, emphasising her words by banging on the notice that warned the conductors to look back for intending passengers with her umbrella as she did so. She took his

number and said she would report him.

When, after my father's death, and during my mother's stay in the sanatorium, I stayed with Grandmother I became aware of the rift between her and Grandfather. In retrospect it is easy to understand the basic cause of the hostility between them. Grandfather's ancestors had belonged to the craftsman class at least since the end of the eighteenth century and perhaps earlier. He took great pride in his work but had no ambition beyond making a comfortable living. Grandmother was very different; the ex-servant had strong social ambitions and a determination to rise in the world. At the same time Grandfather's business was declining, his craft no longer in great demand. He took refuge in the pub or sometimes went to his allotment. I remember once he went up the stairs from the basement kitchen, her shouting after him, 'And don't forget you owe me two pounds!'

He shouted back, 'And two you won't get – that's four!'

Grandmother had a favourite saying which I have never heard

anyone else use, 'If you've a goose, you get a goose and if you haven't got a goose, you get it taken off you.' She was determined to be one of the people who had a goose.

Grandmother's basement kitchen was the most comfortable and cosiest room I have ever been in. There was an area outside the front window, covered by a grating that made a cling clang sound when people walked over it. This room served as both kitchen and dining room. In the centre was a huge mahogany dining table; I used to enjoy winding the handle to extend it at mealtimes. Against the wall opposite the window stood a mahogany press where the tablecloths and cutlery were kept. There were shelves holding bound copies of magazines above the cupboard part. I liked to help polish the blackleaded fireplace and shine the steel fender and the hinges of the oven. Grandmother often gave me the job of laying the table. She insisted on exact precision with all the cutlery and cruets laid out like soldiers on a parade ground. Ceremony and formality were very dear to my grandmother's heart.

One of my many faults was eating too quickly. Grandmother was a superb cook and all her food was delicious. She had an oblique and humorous way of reproving me; 'Don't you like your dinner?' 'Yes, Grandmother it's lovely.' 'Oh, I thought you were trying to gobble it down quickly because you didn't like the taste.'

Grandmother made her girdle scones on a girdle placed over the fire. They were so enjoyable I found it very difficult to take my time. 'Are you eating the scones?' 'Yes Grandmother, they're champion.' 'Oh, I thought you were posting letters.'

After a meal Grandfather would enjoy a pipe of tobacco. He relaxed in his armchair by the fire with his long-stemmed churchwarden pipe. Grandmother disapproved of smoking in the kitchen but on this point Grandfather refused to budge, and relished what Grandmother called 'that stinking thing'.

I enjoyed my stay at Grandmother's. Both my grandparents treated me very well and I was much closer to my Uncle Willie than I ever was to my own father. Every Sunday, when the weather, was fine Uncle Willie took me for long walks over the Town Moor or to Jesmond Dene where he would buy me a glass of sarsparilla. At times, when passing a pub, he would bring me a glass of lemonade to drink outside while he popped in for a quick one, as he called it. For a while I thought 'a quick one' was some special kind of drink. Occasionally, as a special treat, we went on the train to Whitley Bay for a walk along the sea front where he had his quick one at a pub near the promenade. I was always very fond of Uncle Willie and had great admiration for his skill as a craftsman.

After leaving Lovaine Place I saw Grandmother only once more and that was when she was dying. She summoned us all, as if by Royal Command, to see us for the last time. She was sitting propped up with pillows and looking just as imperious as ever. The pommets of her cheeks were still rosy and her face set with its usual composure. She was wearing a cap like the wolf wore in the illustration of Red Riding Hood. Two weeks later she died.

Early Days in Gateshead

My mother was cleaning the window of the front room at 262 Bensham Road in Gateshead. She was standing half-way up a stepladder, polishing the glass with circular movements of the chamois leather. It squeaked on the glass. I stood at the foot of the ladder, clutching the sackcloth apron she wore over her long black skirt. This is my earliest memory apart from a very vague recollection of a soldier kneeling on one knee as he mends the wheel of my pram. I can see the picture, but everything is blurred and indistinct like a badly focused photograph.

Our home was an upstairs flat, built, as were all the other Victorian houses in the neighbourhood, of dull, begrimed, red brick but with quite imposing bay windows with handsome ashlar surrounds in sandstone. All the houses in the terrace were built on ground a few feet higher than street level and had stone steps leading from the token front garden, with its small but respectable cast-iron railings, down to the pavement.

I often stood on a little stool at the front room window with my arms resting on the window sill, observing the road below with the rapt concentration of a child. Most of the traffic on the busy Bensham Road was still horse-drawn. There were two-wheeled flat carts, cumbersome, tall-sided two wheelers and flat four-wheelers all struggling up the bank with the carters cracking whips to urge on the horses. I thought the brewers' drays, drawn by pairs of glossy horses with enormous hooves that slithered and sparked on the cobbles and gleaming brass work on their harness, a wonderful sight. The bowler-hatted driver, perched high on his seat with a tarpaulin over his knees and a whip in his hand, looked like a king. Rington's tea vans had a particular appeal for me. I admired the

gracefully curved
shafts and 'Rington's
Tea' painted in gilt
lettering on the dark
green sides of the van.
Later, when I was a
little older, I used to
follow them and steal
a ride by perching on
the little round iron
step at the back where
the driver stood to
open the doors.

My father
disapproved of my
going into the 'front
room' as it was always
called, but Mother had no objection. I think she was happy
knowing where I was while she got on with her work. I liked best
to look out of the window about dusk when I could watch the
lamplighter turning up the gas at the top of the lamp-posts with a
long pole and see pools of yellowish light forming round the glass
cage that housed the mantles. The tram-cars fascinated me. They
lurched and clattered down the bank, the huge, single lamp at the
front of the tram a great, cyclopean, gleaming eye. At times the
trolley wheel on the overhead wires sent out blue lightning-like
flashes. On its way up the bank the tram sometimes lost traction;
steel turning uselessly on steel. The conductor had to seek sand
from a nearby iron sandbox to strew under the wheels. The
clattering, clumsy thing would then grind slowly on amid showers
of sparks.

Soon after the five o'clock steam whistles sounded in their

amazing chorus from the hundreds of factories crowding the banks of the Tyne, I would watch the men streaming home from work. Their different heights and gaits made it appear, from my vantage point, as if they were bobbing up and down. Most of the men were dressed alike with flat caps, mufflers and dirty raincoats flapping about their knees. They carried bait-tins (lunch-boxes) under one arm. Newsboys dashed down the road, often in bare feet, shouting an unintelligible sound which meant 'Chronicle'.

Most of my time was spent in the living room which was also dining room and kitchen. There was a gas oven in the scullery, but Mother preferred to cook in the fire oven where she baked all our bread. Mother used to allow me to stand on the table to light the gas mantle. She would turn on the gas, hand me a wooden taper lighted at the fire and I would put it to the mantle to hear it go pop.

Sometimes Mother made what she called a 'tasty bite' for my supper, a Welsh Rarebit of cheese, onions and milk heated in a saucepan and poured over a piece of bread, or if the oven was still hot from baking she would bake an onion and top it with butter. After supper she would read to me. This was when I first experienced the thrill of a story. She read from a book by Joseph Hocking about a man being smuggled out of jail by pretending to be dead and being carried out for burial. I have forgotten all the other details, but I remember very clearly the excitement I felt. She read stories from the Brothers Grimm and Hans Andersen. I have a vivid memory of a nightmare I had after hearing about the cat with eyes as big as saucers. I dreamt about an enormous cat, which somehow went between the wooden rollers of the mangle standing in the scullery, and emerged, perfectly flat apart from its head and huge eyes, to leap upon my bed. I woke screaming with horror.

I remember playing under the table. Over the table I would put a large cloth that reached to the floor, I'd gather all the cushions, put them underneath and crawl inside. I can recall the feeling of intense happiness I experienced as I sat there in my nest. I could hear Mother busy with various tasks in the scullery but I seemed somehow to be in a different world. I was reluctant to come out and back to reality even for meals.

The cobbled lane at the back of our house was a place of great interest but also of fear. Directly opposite our back door there was a jam factory with big red doors where carts would load. The lane was always scented with the smell of boiling jam. A neighbour told Mother that rats sometimes fell into vats of boiling jam and were fished out and thrown into the lane. I believed this tale but never saw any candied rats.

The coalman with his two-wheeled flat cart came down the lane shouting 'roundy coal'. He wore a coal sack with a corner pushed in like a monk's cowl over his head. Mother would send me to the fish man with a plate to buy a pennyworth of herrings. He had a wooden wrist with a hook in it making him look like pirate but he could scoop up the herrings very deftly. He used to shout 'caller harn', (fresh herring) as he drove his cart down the lane. The rag-and-bone man alerted people to his presence with blasts on his tin trumpet before shouting hoarsely 'balloons for rags'. His handcart was gaily decorated with inflated balloons and coloured celluloid windmills tied to upright canes at the front of his cart. When I was sent with rags, I had to ask for a donkey stone in return. This was a soft yellow stone used for cleaning the front door steps, a sacred domestic ritual on Tyneside. I had to forego the pleasure of the balloon or windmill.

A flight of stone steps with a wooden banister led down from the scullery to the tiny back yard where Mother hung washing out to dry. Here was the coalhouse and the privy, called the 'netty' in the north. Ashes and rubbish were also tipped into the netty. I always ventured very warily from the backyard into the lane.

Fierce, stray dogs roamed there and a gang of big lads from meaner streets nearer the river prowled round and picked up any articles left unattended. It was said that they occasionally snatched washing from a clothesline. These back lane bandits would enter the lane at the top end and bang with a stick on each door they passed. Cats would make frantic leaps to safety, clawing over the back yard walls, and youngsters like myself scuttled to security through our own doors.

One morning curiosity overcame my fear as I watched them opening and shutting the doors used for cleaning out the netties and peeping inside as they passed. Arriving at our downstairs neighbour's door, one lad shouted 'Here's one!' Another took aim with a catapult and fired at the exposed backside. The occupant gave a loud howl of pain and the gang dashed off laughing and yelling with glee down the lane and round the corner.

I ran back up our backyard stairs immediately to tell Mother of this strange event. She listened and then asked me who the victim was. Then, realizing that that I would hardly be able to recognise the occupant in the circumstances, she twisted her mouth into strange shapes, vainly trying to hold back her laughter, feeling I suppose, that it was wrong to laugh at such an uncouth prank. At last she could contain herself no more and, as always when she laughed heartily, she held her left side with one hand over the other and she became helpless, leaning back in the chair with tears in her eyes. I think what made the episode so funny for Mother was that the woman downstairs, a large imposing person, full of her own importance, was her landlady, and Mother had assumed that she was the victim.

When I became a little older Mother used to send me on errands to the nearby shops. In the grocer's I was fascinated by the white-jacketed assistants slicing bacon in the machine, cutting hunks of cheese with a wire and delving for chunks of butter from barrels with the staves broken open. Sacks of barley, lentils and split peas stood at one side with their tops neatly rolled down. The assistants scooped, weighed and deftly folded packets of required amounts. I loved the rich smell of coffee beans being roasted in a revolving cylinder in the window. I fetched milk from the dairy across the road. The interior was all white tiled and large zinc churns stood behind the counter. The lady serving would dip in the measure, pour the milk into my jug and then add about a tablespoon saying, 'And there's a drop for the cat'.

My favourite shop was the newsagent's where comics were sold. It stood close by the dairy and I used to balance the jug of milk on the narrow windowsill while I read as much as possible from the comics displayed in the window. They were fastened by a clothes peg to a string stretched across the window, some of them sideways, and I had to crane my neck to read them. The titles had a magical appeal for me. *Chips, Funny Wonder, Comic Cuts.* One was printed on a pale blue paper and another was straw coloured. I loved the adventures of a pair of loveable tramps called Weary Willie and Tired Tim. These comics were, I think, all the more appealing because my father, following the strict dictates of the Plymouth Brethren, had forbidden them. When I had a penny to spend I would dash over the road to buy a comic. Mother took my side in this illicit reading, but made sure I hid the comics under a pile of newspapers kept in the corner cupboard for lighting the fire.

Father had been a Wesleyan when he and Mother were married, but by the time I was born he had left the relatively jolly Wesleyans and became a Plymouth Brother. He was the survivor of twins; his twin brother was stillborn. Though small, Father was well proportioned with refined features and slightly bulging eyes that gave him a serious look. At the beginning of the war he had volunteered for the army but was rejected on fitness grounds.

Instead, he was given a khaki armband to show he had volunteered and was directed to work in Armstrong's ordnance factory in Newcastle as a fitter. When the war was over, he went back to his father's workshop in Pilgrim Street.

Mother told me that when they were first married, Father sang in a choir and played the violin, sometimes in a trio. He also owned a gramophone and was a keen watercolour painter. Unfortunately, when he joined the Brethren, Father gave up these activities and disposed of his gramophone. There was no music in our home. Brethren philosophy could be rather perverse, so perhaps he had given up his pleasures precisely because he enjoyed them. I hardly knew my father. He was a remote figure whose life, when not working, was filled with evangelical pursuits: preaching, prayer meetings and Bible study.

On Sundays my father took me with him to the Brethren services held in the Bewick Hall which was a dance hall on weekdays. Much later I discovered it was named after Thomas Bewick the famous engraver who detested ranters. I remember distinctly the dreary feeling I experience as we walked through the sad, deserted Sunday streets. Father held my hand and I had to run to keep up with him. When we arrived I would help him and others to set out the chairs. The floor was highly polished and a faint smell of perfume, used by the jolly sinners on the previous evening, mingled with the odour of wax polish. Because the floor was so slippery I was always tempted to have a slide on it. One of the elders, a gaunt Scotsman, would admonish me, 'The Lord Jesus would no' like you to do that.'

The Brethren regarded music as a sinful distraction and hymns were sung unaccompanied. A man nicknamed 'The Organ' led the dreary dirges which were mostly about the blood of the lamb. He was a converted professional boxer of immense girth with a very deep and powerful bass voice; his opening notes seemed to drop to the floor and slide along its polished surface. I was rather afraid of this huge man and avoided him as much as possible: perhaps I felt he might give me a punch on the nose for some misdeed.

The sermons were long and arduous. I would wriggle and squirm on my chair and Father would give me a little tap with his hand to make me sit still. After the sermon various members stood up to pray. The rest of the congregation encouraged the speaker with shouts of 'Amen', 'Praise the Lord' and 'Hallelujah', like a boxer being boosted with shouts from his supporters at the ringside.

On one occasion the Brethren were shocked by a scandal in their midst. One of the young newly married Brothers deserted his wife and ran away to London with a girl who was not a member. This scandal provided subject matter for prayers for a long time, but without any result. The erring member never returned.

I can only remember one occasion when Father took me anywhere apart from Bewick Hall and that was to visit a chapel in Newcastle to hear a gypsy horse-thief turned evangelist preach. The reformed horse-thief was a very good turn. He was a big man with a fat belly like the Bewick Hall Organ and he had learned how to present his material in a very dramatic way. With large gestures and timed pauses he told the congregation about his wicked past; how he used to alter the appearance of the stolen horses by clipping their manes and tails and dyeing light coloured patches with dark dye. The Brethren all groaned in unison as he confessed these sins and shouted 'Hallelujah!' and 'Praise the Lord!' when he told them of his conversion and maintained he had never stolen a horse since that day. After this the organ played and the plates were passed round for a collection to help him convert more gypsy horse-thieves.

Off to School

The teacher held up a large piece of card divided into two parts like a domino, 'Now there are five spots and four spots, how many altogether?' Long before I had arrived at an answer, most of the children had their hands up, eager to respond. I hated this silly game with dots. After a while she turned the card to the blank side and asked the same question. This teacher is one of two I remember from Chester Place Infants School where I began my schooling a few months before my fifth birthday. She was, as I remember her, always dressed the same way; a long narrow black skirt, almost touching the ground, and a very dark red blouse that was tight at the wrist and had a ruffled collar enclosing her neck. Her black hair was piled on top of her head and fastened with hairpins.

The second teacher was entirely different; she had fair, bobbed hair, still rare at that time, an open-necked blouse and a short skirt. Usually she had a large wooden knitting needle in her hand which she sometimes used to rap our knuckles if we were inattentive. She had a strange habit of plunging this needle down under her blouse to scratch her chest. I was a complete duffer at mental arithmetic. This second teacher introduced more complicated questions involving money and how many apples could be bought for a certain sum of money.

'Now Tommy,' she would say, 'if apples are five for sixpence' – dip dip went the needle – 'how many can you buy for one shilling and sixpence?' I was lost. As soon as I formed a clear picture of the apples in my mind, the dots disappeared. I made no progress. Most of my classmates stabbed the air eagerly with their hands and called out 'Miss, miss!' I just sat sullenly blank. My seat-mate, a girl with a pigtail who smelled of towels drying on an oven door,

22

bounced up and down excitedly. I had forgotten the original statement. The mistress dipped her needle and scratched furiously. 'Tell him children,' she demanded. The answer came simultaneously in a kind of singsong chant. I did not care and just felt stubborn.

Apart from my troubles with dots and apples, my only other recollection is of the intense boredom of having to sit in the class with children learning the letters of the alphabet and chanting 'A for apple' when I could already read fluently (Mother had taught me to read before I started the infant school at Chester Place). After a year or two at this school I was transferred to Brighton Road School.

The playground at Brighton Road School was a seething mass of boys yelling and cheering. I was grabbed by many hands and thrown skywards. The iron railings round the yard, the red brick school building, the sky and the sea of faces all blurred in my vision as I rolled in the air, dropped and was hoisted high again. Then I suddenly found myself held face down over a concrete

block in the yard with many hands clutching my arms and legs. The tormentors began to chant in unison 'One-er two-er three-er!' Between each count a big lad gave me a whack over the backside with a stick. After ten whacks they let me go. Everyone cheered and the big lads sought another victim to be thrown in the air and hauled to the block. My Mother had sent me to my new school very smartly dressed with an Eton collar and a little bow tie worn over a jacket with specially cut away lapels. The Eton collar and bow tie were snatched away from my neck as I stepped through the gate and I never saw them again. After this initiation I went to school in jersey and shorts, blended in with my fellows and had no more trouble. I attended Brighton Road School for about two years and can remember nothing of any interest.

The Wanderer

As I grew older I developed a great longing to explore the outside world. Whenever I could I would slip away and wander, gazing at anything that attracted my attention. My parents discouraged me from mixing with other children or visiting their houses, and this had made me into a loner. They visited no one and only rarely did anyone visit us. It was only in later years that I pondered how strange it was that Father had five sisters and two brothers, yet none of them came to see us and nor did he, as far as I know, ever go to see them. This isolation sharpened my yearning for life outside.

At the top end of Bensham Bank there was a large grassy space named Windmill Hills after the windmills which had previously stood there. It provided a playground and a place where I could run about and observe whatever was going on. From the top of the

hills, I could see Newcastle on the opposite bank of the River Tyne like a picture map with the church steeples, factory chimneys and tall buildings clearly visible. Ship sirens hooting for the Swing Bridge to open sounded very close.

From the highest point of the Hills, men threw racing pigeons from wickerwork baskets into the air and boys clung on to kite lines made from oddments of string. Where iron railings marked the boundary, girls played endless games of houses in tents made of sackcloth impaled on the railing points and weighted on the ground with large stones. They used empty tins and utensils salvaged from rubbish heaps to make cakes and loaves of bread from mud. Pairs of girls twirled skipping ropes and chanted 'Raspberry, strawberry, marmalade, jam' and as the speed increased, 'Salt, mustard, cayenne pepper' and played 'Hitchie Dabber', called Hopscotch elsewhere. Boys and girls ran about with iron hoops called 'gawls' which they rolled along with the help of an iron hook.

I envied the boys who had home-made bogies to ride down the concrete paths; the bogies were made from a single plank with two small wheels at the front on a moveable axle and two large ones at the back. They whizzed downhill with a fine turn of speed.

Near the road stood a four-sided shelter of wood and glass. Here on fine days the ex-servicemen congregated. Some had an empty jacket sleeve, pinned to the upper arm with a safety pin, and others an empty trouser leg pinned to the thigh. One man was blind and used to tow his crippled friend up the bank to the shelter, holding out his white stick for his friend to grip. The crippled man helped himself along with his rubber ferruled walking stick and acted as navigator shouting out directions to the blind man. All these men were dressed alike in shabby navy blue suits, white or pale blue mufflers and flat grey caps. They sat in the shelter smoking clay pipes or Woodbines and spat, talked and laughed. I was very curious about the pink racing paper in which they were so interested. I would stand and stare until one of them chased me away by pretending to pick up a stone to throw at me. About eleven o'clock they would set off for the pub over the road, The Hen and Chickens, the blind man towing his pal.

The Bensham Picture House stood close to the Hills and I never passed without loitering for a while to look at the stills displayed in the foyer. I would gaze in wonder at the pictures of Tom Mix the cowboy on his white horse, Fatty Arbuckle, comic policemen, and other people in strange costumes. While enjoying the stills I always kept an eye out for any of the Brethren, particularly the gaunt Scotsman, a Jeremiah in a black Homberg hat, batwing collar, black tie and a long black coat. If ever I spotted one of the Brethren, I dashed away with my head down and pretended not to see him.

I managed only twice to beat Father's ban; once when the school arranged a visit to see 'The Covered Wagon' and once, when, on a very rare visit to Grandmother's house, my Aunt Flossie, who must have sympathised with my situation, took me to the cinema to see *Shoulder Arms*. I became a Charlie Chaplin fan forever. Mother told me I used to do Chaplin acts to amuse her for a long time afterwards.

When I was about eight or nine I became interested in crossing the river to the Newcastle side. On Saturday mornings Father would give me what he called my Saturday penny. I was always torn with indecision how to spend it; I could, by using the free Swing Bridge, have the whole penny to spend, but I enjoyed crossing the High Level Bridge for a halfpenny toll. I could walk over or have a halfpenny ride on the horse-drawn brake. I loved the ride but it did not last very long so I usually decided to walk. Then I would be able to loiter and look down at the river and perhaps see a ship passing below. Sometimes, as the bridge reverberated with the roar of the trains overhead, I would give myself a thrill of horror by imagining what would happen if the bridge collapsed and everything, including myself, hurtled into the river far below.

Near the Newcastle end of the bridge, an organ grinder had his pitch. A tiny monkey in a bright red jacket stood on top of the organ beside the tin cup used for receiving coppers. It had sad brown eyes and was always shivering. A chain from the shaft of the organ was fastened to a leather collar round its neck. The only tune I remember the grinder playing was *Daisy Bell*.

Though I did not know it until many years later, my great-great-Grandfather had a blacksmith's shop not far from the bridge end at Newcastle, and there had founded the firm of Bell Brothers. Also quite nearby and at the same period, 1812, Thomas Bewick had his engraver's workshop.

Castle Stairs, several flights of stone steps with an iron hand-rail, provided a short cut from near the end of the High Level to the quayside and the approach to the Swing Bridge. About half way down, a clogger worked in his tiny workshop. I would stop awhile to watch him making clogs at his bench in front of the window. If I heard a ship hooting and the warning bell sounding, I would hurry down to get on to the bridge in time to watch the ship passing through the channel left when the centre part of the bridge swung round.

I would return home by way of Bottle Bank, a narrow, very steep cobbled road which led up into Gateshead from the Swing Bridge. The horses sweated and their shoes struck sparks as they struggled upwards, their sides lathered white where the harness touched them. Coming down the road, the drivers would put iron brake shoes under the wheels to lock them and hold back the carts as the horses slithered down, front legs splayed. Bottle Bank had a very strange atmosphere; the houses and shops were extremely old and some of the shop windows were of a peculiar shape. One of

them, at the bottom end where the High Level soared high
overhead, had a bow window where copies of the *Police News*
were displayed. The covers always showed drawings of famous
murders with all the graphic details. This shop sold second-hand
comics for one halfpenny or exchanged one of his for two of
yours. If I decided not to buy a comic, I would call in the shop
higher up and buy a multi-layered gobstopper, each layer a
different colour. Near this shop was a pub called the Goat with a
large model of a goat on an iron bracket above the door. Mother
told me that her stepmother, to whom we always referred as
Granny Newton, had once been a barmaid in the Goat.

  On my way home from Bottle Bank I passed some waste
ground given over to hoardings for posters. I was always interested
in these; a man with a large tin of Andrews Liver Salts in his hip
pocket is searching in his open suitcase and saying, 'I must have
left it behind'. A sailing ship is moving across an unruffled blue sea
leaving a white wake, 'Out of the blue comes the whitest wash'

(Reckitts Blue). 'Now he's in a fine pickle', a dog is bespattered with pickle from the Pan Yan pickle jar it has knocked over. A happy looking man in gaily striped pyjamas is sailing out to sea perched on a huge Bovril bottle, 'Prevents that sinking feeling'. A pig is pulling a truck piled high with Palethorpe's sausages, 'Drawing its own conclusion'.

My wanderings were not always devoid of danger. 'Green peas or barley?' I would find myself cornered by a small group of boys armed with basters, tightly rolled balls of paper tied round with string leaving one string long to swing it by. I knew both answers would be wrong and I would have to curl up with crossed arms to protect my face as the blows landed on my head and shoulders. At election times the question was, 'Who are you voting for?' I learned in time that the best way to deal with basters was to grab them, entangle the strings and so make my escape. At times gangs of boys who found a loner too good an opportunity to miss would attack me. I developed an unorthodox means of defence; when knocked to the ground I would stay down and, pivoting about on my backside, could kick and use my arms to grab ankles and bring down an assailant. Once, a boy whose ankle I had grabbed fell awkwardly and broke his leg. His Father came to see mine to complain. I sat on the fender beside the fire with my head bowed, my arms about my knees. My Father mistook my attitude for contrition. I was surly and defiant really because I felt I had been wrongly accused and could not find the words to justify myself. Father insisted I call at the boy's home to say I was sorry. To my surprise his parents were not at all vindictive and the boy with his leg in plaster sat grinning at me.

Once on my way home from the Windmill Hills a lad leaning over the high boundary wall shouted down to me, 'Hi kidda!' I looked up and he threw down a soil-laden turf on to my upturned face. I stumbled home half blinded, my eyes stinging.

A Pennyworth of Pot-stuff

'He's like a tuppeny rabbit' Sally said. 'A lovely little rabbit.' She held my brother Norman high in the air with her hands under his armpits after bathing him in a little zinc bath in front of the fire. Norman was a few days old and I was nearly seven. Sally was a dear friend of Mother. She was small and plump, full of kindness and good humour. She belonged to the Brethren but was one of those people who would be the same lovable person regardless of sect or religion. I was always delighted to see her and I would run downstairs to answer the door when she called, to be greeted with a cuddle and a kiss on the forehead. Mother was still ill in bed and dear Sally had taken over the running of our home.

My brother Norman's birth had little effect on my life except that Mother's attention was mostly on the baby and I was able to dodge out of the house more easily and spend even more time on my wanderings and explorations. I discovered Saltwell Park and would go there on Sunday afternoons if I could escape, to listen to the band playing, a tremendous treat for a young boy whose life was devoid of all music. I once was lucky and found myself in some street where a Highland band was playing and marching along. I joined the great crowd of urchins following behind and was filled with glee and excitement. I must have caused my mother much worry and unease by these long absences.

Two years after Norman's birth my father died. He died from pleurisy brought on by receiving a soaking in Durham where he spent Saturday afternoons in the market-place selling books. I knew nothing about his bookselling activities, but probably they were of a religious nature.

I remember weeping when told of Father's death and Sally

taking me on her knee to comfort me, but he was such a remote person to me that I was not deeply afflicted.

Mother became ill after Father's death and was sent to a sanatorium in Wolsingham in County Durham for six months. I went to stay with my grandmother in Lovaine Place, Newcastle, and our dear friend Sally looked after my brother Norman. My Uncle Willie came to seek me and took me to my grandmother's. I was disappointed at having to ride there on the crossbar of Uncle Willie's bicycle, I had hoped at least for a tram ride.

But, on my return to Gateshead, life was set to take a turn for the worse.

Some months after my homecoming my cousin Tom Newton and I found ourselves walking along Windy Nook Road with an inverted kitchen table on our heads. We had tied a clothesline round the legs to form a cage in which were piled baskets, dishes, bedclothes, pots and pans, cushions and various odds and ends. We had spent most of the day carrying bed ends, mattresses and chairs. The table cage was our last load.

After leaving Bensham we moved, first of all, to a house near Kell's Lane, but having heard of one with an even cheaper rent in Windy Nook we were changing homes yet again. The house at Windy Nook was the end one of a long terrace. It contained a bedroom, a living room-cum-kitchen with a fire oven and gaslight and a little yard at the back with a coal house and a netty. We were lucky to have gaslight as many of the houses in the neighbourhood were still using paraffin lamps. Beyond our house there was a large stretch of unused ground where miners had built gaily painted pigeon lofts, called duckets or crees, where they pampered their pigeons for racing. Miners also walked their skinny whippets on this ground, played quoits and sometimes held gambling schools of pitch and toss.

Mother was destitute after Father's death and, as my

grandfather had not paid into the state insurance scheme on behalf of his three sons, she was not entitled to a widow's pension and was forced to seek help from the Board of Guardians. Grandfather contributed three shillings a week, but, as this was taken into account by the board when assessing Mother's income, she was no better off. Her life at this time must have been very unhappy; she dreaded 'not being able to manage', a phrase often on her lips. I think that her greatest fear was that illness would strike again and that Norman and I would be placed in a children's home.

Mother had no friends in Windy Nook, no one to whom she could unburden her troubles and fears. After Father's death she went no more to the Brethren meetings and none of them visited us, nor did Father's brothers and sisters call upon us, or communicate in any way as far as I am aware.

Mother had a brother, Tom Newton (father of cousin Tom), living in Deckham about a mile away from Windy Nook, but he was almost a stranger to us, as they had not been brought up together. I do not think they had even visited each other when we lived in Bensham, but it was Uncle Tom's wife, my Aunt Dora, who proved to be the friend in need. Uncle Tom and Aunt Dora lived in an upstairs flat in a terrace of red brick houses called Caris Street. My uncle had rigged up an ingenious system with cord and pulleys so that the front door could be opened without going downstairs.

One of my clearest memories of this house is my Aunt Dora on her baking days. She always made some of the near-mystical bread of the North East called 'Stotty Cake' which is baked on the bottom shelf of the oven. Those of us present sat round the table like nestlings agape for our piece of stotty cake. At last Aunty would open the oven door and bring out the golden brown flat round of bread, about eighteen inches in diameter and one and a half inches thick, slightly wrinkled and with dark brown scorch

marks. We ate it hot, almost straight from the oven. Aunt Dora
would hold it with an oven cloth against herself cutting it into
slices. She would daub each slice with margarine and hand a piece
to each of us in turn and we would blow on it for a few seconds to
cool it sufficiently to put in our mouths. We could eat it faster
than she could cut it.

My Uncle Tom and Aunt Dora Newton had eight children, five
girls and three boys. I hardly knew the two eldest girls; when we
lived in Windy Nook, Elsie and Jenny had left school and were out
at work. Olive and Winnie were roughly my own age. Eva would
be born in 1929. Two of the boys, Andy and Jack, were younger
than myself and Tom a couple of years older. I greatly admired my
cousin Tom. He attended the local Grammar School, a rare
distinction, and was learning to speak French. Even more worthy
of adulation in my eyes, he could play the banjo and sing comic
songs. In fine weather he and some of his pals used to make a tent
of sackcloth on some vacant ground adjoining Caris Street. They
built a wood fire on which they baked potatoes while Tom
entertained with his banjo and songs such as *Paddy McGinty's
Goat, Ivan Skavinsky Skavar* and *The Spaniard That Blighted my
Life.*

Tom was very resourceful and had collected the money to buy
his banjo by doing odd jobs for people in more prosperous parts of
the town, beating carpets, scouring back yards or any job for a few
coppers.

When Tom took me with him to the public library in
Swinburne Street, I was astounded. By some strange irony, many
of the streets in the poorer parts of Gateshead were named after
poets. J.B. Priestley commented on this in his *English Journey*.
Until then I had been unaware that there were such places as
public libraries. The fee to join was one penny for three years,
surely the finest pennyworth ever. We were not allowed to see the

actual books, but had to choose a book by scanning typed lists of authors and book titles numbered and displayed in a large glass fronted case. Having chosen a book, you had to quote the number at the desk to find out if it was available. There was no way of knowing whether a book was in or out, so if your choice was unavailable, you had to choose again. With Tom as my mentor I discovered Henty, Marryat, Wynne-Reed, Fenimore Cooper and Defoe's *Robinson Crusoe*.

When the miner's strike was on and coal was extremely scarce, Tom and I went what was called 'scratting for coal' on the huge waste heaps of grey slag. All day long the narrow black earth lane, lined with dusty hawthorn bushes, leading to the slag heaps, was filled with people going or returning with their sacks of coal. Some used home-made barrows, old prams, pushchairs and bicycles while others carried sacks on their backs using a rope belt padded with cloth where it pressed on the forehead and fastened behind the sack to take some of the weight. Tom and I had only the essentials; a sackcloth apron we held with one hand in which we deposited the pieces of coal before transferring them to our sacks, and headbands to assist us in carrying the full sacks home. Our finger ends soon became sore from shifting pieces of slag and probing among the small stuff to pick up tiny pieces of coal that

lay underneath. By late afternoon we had collected as much as we could carry and we joined the stream of people wending homewards along the black path among the prams with squeaky axles and the bicycles with buckled wheels that rubbed against the frame at every turn, all laden with our precious gleanings. Some. like Tom and myself, used the headband method and staggered a little until forced to rest awhile by the path side.

One day when we went to Heworth intending to scrat for coal, we found everyone making their way to the pithead instead of the slag heaps. There was an air of excitement and we found that blacklegs would be attempting to enter the pit. We forgot about scratting and followed the crowd.

'Get out of the way you young uns.' A man gave us a clout over the head and a fat woman, wearing a shawl and a man's flat cap said, 'Get away you!'

Tom and I made our way to a slight rise in the ground where we could watch the crowd assembled near the pithead. At first it was quiet with only a rumble of talk, like the sound of people waiting for the appearance of someone of great importance. The noise of shouts and screams of abuse exploded when a Black Maria, followed by mounted police, appeared on the roadway leading to the pit shaft. The crowd surged forwards in an attempt to prevent the Black Maria reaching the pit cage, but the mounted police cleared a way by backing their horses into the crush. As the safetymen in their working gear climbed out of the van to enter the cage, the shouts of 'Blacklegs' from angry faces and cries of abuse blended into one great sound of fury. Some of those at the back of the crowd threw stones and the police horses knocked some men to the ground. The safetymen carrying their lamps darted into the cage, the gate clanged shut and the wheels at the top of the shaft began to turn. The Black Maria with its escort moved away. All was quiet again. Some men went to help the injured and people began to filter away in small groups.

About the same time that Tom and I went scratting for coal, Mother became ill again and I had to do the shopping. I remember her leaning over to write out a list for me on the little table by her bedside. After Father died she had her black hair cut short and it was now a mass of curls that fell about her face as she wrote down the items. Mostly the list was of pennyworths of ingredients to make a dinner. I sought bacon scraps at the grocer's, bones at the butcher's and pennyworths of pot-stuff at the greengrocer's. The pot-stuff varied but was usually a very small onion, a piece of turnip and a small carrot. These, with pinches of various pulses Mother kept in stone jars as a rearguard in her fight against hunger, made wonderful stews or broths. These jars together with others of flour, oatmeal and dripping were like the widow's purse in the Bible story, never allowed to become completely empty, but unfortunately not by supernatural means.

A popular base for making broth was a sheep's head. Some people would send a boy to the slaughterhouse to buy one more cheaply. On his way home with the gory object the boy would sometimes pull up his jersey over his head and holding the sheep's head on top of his own would shout, 'Hi kiddas!' to some unwary children who would scatter in mock horror on beholding the mini-devil. Though Mother did make sheep's head broth occasionally, I was never sent on this gruesome errand.

When Mother was even more than usually hard up, I would go to the pork butcher's to buy a pennyworth of pease pudding to spread on bread for a meal. The pork butcher's window fascinated me; I would stand with my nose flattened against the glass looking at the amazing variety of good things displayed – trays of shiny black pudding and white, some strange objects called penny ducks or ducks with veils on, objects of unknown substance covered with white fat, sausages, red polony and pigs' trotters. At Christmastime a pig's head with an orange stuck in its mouth and sprigs of parsley behind its ears graced the window.

As I stood waiting to be served, like one of the Bisto Kids smelling the steam from the large containers of pease pudding and gravy, I would look longingly at the large joints of roast pork encased in brown crackling, the trays of hot savaloys and the heaps of bread rolls which the butcher dipped on a long fork into the gravy for penny dips or split to make pork sandwiches. I think my idea of heaven then would have been a whole basin of pease pudding to myself with a saveloy sticking in it to use as a scoop.

While Mother was ill in bed she sent me once to the Guardians to draw her weekly allowance. I stood with the people waiting for their turn at the back of the hall. A big man with a spotted bow tie sitting with his assistant behind a trestle table shouted 'The B's!' 'Ye gan noo hinny,' said a woman wearing a black shawl and a man's cap perched on top of her head. I made my way forward and joined the queue in front of the table. I handed the big man Mother's letter. He glanced at the letter and said, 'Where's the certificate boy?' I wondered what kind of certificate he meant and made no answer but just looked blank. His voice rose to a shout with exasperation, 'The medical certificate from the doctor, you stupid boy!'

'Bastard!' The word came out like a stone from a sling. The big man jerked up his head and glared at the crowd of people waiting for their turn, and his assistant stretched out his skinny neck from his celluloid collar like a tortoise. I turned round amazed. Every face was impassive as far as I could see. One woman was holding a shawl over her mouth, but I knew the voice had been a man's. The big man decided in my favour and gave me the money in an envelope. He wagged his pencil at me and said, 'I hope you are telling the truth boy.'

Spuggie, Beany, and other Pals

Mother's illness had delayed my attending my new school for a week or two and, mindful of the tricks played on new-starters, I was rather apprehensive. However I was mostly ignored and soon adjusted. I can remember little of the school except the games in the schoolyard. My favourite was 'Munty Kitty', really, 'Mount the Cuddy', in which boys of one team made a cuddy (a horse) by forming a long line of backs with arms round the middle of the boy in front. One boy had to be the cushion by standing against a wall with the head of the first boy of the cuddy nestling against his belly. The rival team would leap one at a time on to the back of the cuddy and if the cuddy could bear the combined weight while, 'Munty Kitty, Munty Kitty, one two three,' was chanted, the role of the cuddy was taken by the opposing team. If the cuddy collapsed, they had to start all over again. I can still clearly recall the excitement of taking a great leap through the air and landing with a thud on the outstretched backs, hearing the grunts, groans and oaths as the cuddy collapsed and we all crashed to the ground amid a mass of swirling arms and legs and weird smells.

Prisoner's Base, called 'Relievo' in the North, was very popular, as was a game known as Horses and Riders played by groups of three boys, two forming a centaur-like creature ridden by the third. The object was to unseat other riders until only one remained.

I had been only a short while at Sheriff Hill School when a group of us were transferred to a hall in Kell's Lane, which had no playground, or, as far as I know, even a name. I never found why or which method of selection for transfer had been used. I hated the place, as did all the boys. I detested the master, a tall thin man who attempted to terrorize us by caning and cuffing. He was obsessed by weights and measures. He used to give mental arithmetic tests involving a knowledge of pecks and bushels, rods, poles and perches, fathoms and furlongs. He used to cane all the boys who scored less that a given figure out of twenty questions. At first I went out dutifully to receive a swipe from the cane, but I soon reasoned that since I was certain to be caned anyway, I may as well sit still and let him find out for himself that I had less than the required number of correct answers. I also copied answers from other boys. I would gaze into infinity and mumble my lips as if working out the answers, but in reality straining my eyeballs to catch a glimpse of my neighbour's work.

This same teacher used to place an upturned bucket or his trilby hat on his desk and, when the monitor had given out pencils and paper, he would say, 'Draw that.' Then he would wander among the desks clouting boys who had made mistakes over the head. Once when I was drawing his trilby hat, I drew the bow on the hat band which could not be seen from where I was sitting; he gave me a fierce blow on the side of my head that knocked me out of my desk on to the floor.

I have retained a very clear memory of a podgy, medium-sized boy nicknamed Spuggy, the north country word for sparrow, who had a great gift for comic movement and facial expressions; he could contort his face into preposterous grimaces and twist his body into curious shapes to amuse the class. He used this gift to its greatest effect when he was being punished and had found it to be a powerful weapon. When about to be caned he would retreat, jutting out his backside, making awful faces and moving his forearm back and forth like a piston as the teacher attempted to overtake him and land a blow on the hand. Eventually the cane would make contact on Spuggy's finger ends when he would thrust his smarting hand under his armpit and hop about the room yelling, 'Ooh ya, ooh ya!' all the while distorting his face into exaggerated expressions of pain.

Sometimes when the teacher became exasperated, he would thrust Spuggy over a desk to cane his backside. When this happened Spuggy would hop about the room clutching his behind with both hands while shouting 'Ooh ya, ooh ya!' and pulling awful faces. Several of the lads were unable to control their laughter and would be hauled out for caning. In spite of the pain they continued laughing with tears of mirth and pain running down their faces. Spuggy gained great esteem by these performances. I can still see the bare-footed podgy boy in a ragged green jersey, as he pranced about performing his act of defiance by ridicule.

Once a mother came to school to complain about the severity of her son's caning and a rowdy scene took place in the corridor. We climbed on the desks to peer over the lower panes of frosted glass and were delighted to see the mother threatening the master with an umbrella and heard the woman scream at him, 'And what will ye dee, ye skinny get?' The words became a catch phrase with us and inevitably the teacher became known as 'The skinny get'.

There was no schoolyard or playground at this school, so we spent our breaks in the street. One very warm day the whisper went round at morning break, 'The Gut this after.' The Gut, as we called it, was a small tributary of the River Tyne where we used to swim. As we repeated this message to each other, excitement took over and instead of lining up for school after dinner, we all set off running down the road leading to Low Fell station and what was then the country. Part of our way led us down a footpath with a high fence on one side where the sun shining through the trees behind the fence formed a pattern of shadows on the path. We leapt up to catch hold of lower branches as we passed.

In a field we saw some pit ponies that had been brought to the surface because of the miners' strike. They galloped about in the sunshine exulting in their freedom. Our noisy approach seemed to excite them and some rolled over on their backs waving their legs in the air.

We ran whooping with delight to one of our favourite swimming places where there was a bend in the river and a tree with an overhanging branch grew on the bank side. Soon the river was full of noisy happy boys and the air was full of the sounds of plops and splashes as we dived, jumped or were thrown in. We took it in turns to climb he tree and worm our way along the overhanging branch. I remember the feeling of excitement I experienced as I let go of the branch, the strange sound in my ears as I went to the bottom and kicked myself to the surface again. When we were tired of swimming, we lay on the bank in the warmth of the sunshine, practised cartwheels or walking on our hands. I suppose we were punished for this mass truancy, but I have no recollection of it. Perhaps authority preferred to ignore it.

During the winter following the mass truancy, the bullying teacher slipped on a slide we had made in the street. The next morning he was not at school. I never found out what had happened to him and did not see him again. I still had fresh in my memory the savage and undeserved blow that had sent me flying out of my desk.

One of the most memorable of my friends in this school was a lad nicknamed Beany. He was above average height, pigeon chested with very narrow shoulders. He was always ragged and usually barefoot whatever the weather. I think his mother was dead or had left his father, with whom he lived in a very dirty, smelly cottage. Though often the butt of pranks and jokes, he was very popular with all of us.

Beany was the hungriest boy I ever knew. In springtime, when the hawthorn leaves were new and fresh, he browsed on them like a sheep. He called them bread and cheese. I tried them but did not like the taste. Whenever he saw orange peel or an apple core lying in the gutter he would pick it up and eat with great relish.

One day when he and I were passing along the road where the houses were, by our standards, very high class, he spied some crusts from breakfast toast left on the window ledge to feed the birds, and darted over the front garden to grab them. He stuffed some into his mouth and, holding the rest in his hands, dashed back to the road. The house owner must have seen him through the window for he came out of the side door and began throwing stones at Beany. We fled along the road with stones bouncing about our ankles as we ran. Beany was, as usual, barefooted and was wearing a jacket someone had given him which was far too big and fastened with a safety pin and a piece of thick string around his waist. He looked like a fugitive scarecrow.

Many of the women in the neighbourhood felt sorry for Beany and would give him a slice of bread and jam or dripping. He called all the women 'Ma' and would say, 'Thank y' Ma' with a big grin of pleasure showing his yellow teeth and set off along the road eating the bread and licking his fingers. Mother always referred to him as 'that poor bairn'. He was, in an expression of the time, 'left to God and good neighbours'. Many years later, during the war, I met a soldier who told me that Beany had been killed at Dunkirk.

A lad by the nickname of Richie influenced me a great deal during my stay at the nameless school. We had a mutual love of reading and he introduced me to the *Magnet* and the *Gem*. We also read avidly other boys' weeklies such as the *Rover*, *Adventure* and the *Boy's Magazine*, but the *Magnet* remained our firm favourite. The *Magnet* and other comics cost twopence new, but we could buy second-hand copies for one penny or, in the swap shop, exchange two for one. Usually we swapped with each other. *Magnet*s were like marbles and cigarette cards, a kind of currency.

Richie was a strongly-built lad with a freckled face. He was a natural leader and organiser and was always full of plans for making money, and he knew all the places where it was possible to obtain a few coppers.

Our first ploy was gathering newspapers door to door to exchange for a couple of scoops of chips. The chip shop, made of black corrugated iron, stood on a piece of ground near our house. A funnel at one end belched out smoke and sparks, and a glow of friendly light came through the window from the paraffin lamp hung on a roof beam inside. We enjoyed the rich promise provided by the sound of bubbling fat, the sizzling of newly cut chips dropping into the fat and the enticing smell of chips, fritters and fish frying.

'Put a few scranchions in, Mister,' we would plead when he shovelled chips into the half sheet of newspaper cupped in his other hand. The scranchions were the small pieces of batter and tiny pieces of chips skimmed from the fat and kept in a separate compartment. On cold dark nights we used to stand against the rear wall of the chip shop warming our backsides and passing the paper of chips back and forth, each taking one chip at a time and finally a pinch or two of scranchions. Eventually the owner was stacked up with newspapers and refused to take any more.

Richie introduced me to the custom of frequenting the road near church or chapel entrances when a wedding was taking place, usually St Mary's, Gateshead Parish Church, near the river. It was the custom for the groom to throw handfuls of coppers from the window of the ribbon-bedecked taxi with the pair of old boots dangling behind for luck as it drove away. We would run alongside shouting, 'Hoy a ha'penny oot' and watching for the hand with the money to emerge from the window. A mass of boys were immediately pushing, shoving, charging each other to grab coins where they could. Whether to scramble for the first throwout or to

continue running alongside the taxi hoping for a second one
provided a moment of tormenting indecision. I and my pals always
kept a sharp look out for people waiting outside any church or
chapel; for the bride and groom to emerge so we could join in the
scramble for coppers and the chant of, 'Hoy a ha'penny oot'.

My pal Richie initiated me into another way of obtaining
pennies. When the small passenger ships sailed for Scandinavian
ports from Newcastle quayside, the foreign passengers would
amuse themselves by throwing the remnants of their small change
onto the quayside and watching the boys scramble for the coins.
One day just as I bent down to pick up a penny an enormous hand
grabbed my neck; a policeman held me in one hand and another
urchin in the other and he marched us off clear of the quayside.
The other boys had seen him and escaped. I thought he was taking
us to prison, but, after marching us clear he let us go with a mere
token clout over the back of the head. I suppose the real reason
was for safety in case we pushed each other into the river while
fighting for the coins. Richie and I had managed, however, to
collect a few pence each before the policeman came.

A general dealer's shop stood in a short
street which edged the
waste ground where the
corrugated iron
chip shop stood.
We were often
torn with
indecision where to
spend our pennies.
While the chip shop
offered the most for the
least, we sometimes were
attracted by the sweets. This

shop sold everything from paraffin oil, which stood in a large container in the middle of the floor, to tiny packets of tea and cocoa. The fat, blowsy woman who kept the shop would also sell half a loaf or a single Wild Woodbine cigarette for one halfpenny. A large portion of the counter and the shop window contained a selection of cheap sweets: everlasting strips of toffee, gob stoppers, cinder toffee, soda fountains, sherbet dabs, lemonade crystals, liquorice root and tiger nuts and, most attractive in my eyes, Dickman's delicious snowballs, one halfpenny each but unfortunately gone in a flash and only to be considered on very rare occasions.

My favourite pennyworth was the Saturday matinee which we called the Penny Scrush at the cinemas. The nearest to Windy Nook was the Corona in Felling. Long before the doors opened, hordes of lads used to gather, all fighting for a place near the door. Any lad unwisely wearing a cap would have it snatched from his head and flung into the roadway. When the doors did open the 'checkie' would use his peaked cap like a flail, vainly trying to beat back the writhing, pushing mob into an orderly line.

Once inside, the hubbub was enormous; boys shouted the names of their pals they had been separated from during the melée outside, and fought for priority over certain seats. Audience participation was a very important element of the Penny Scrush. We shouted advice to the heroes on the screen, warned them of impending danger by yelling, 'Nit nit, look oot!' and booed the villains with all our might. We disapproved strongly of any love interest and expressed our disgust by stamping on the floor and delivering great smacking kisses on the backs of our hands. If a film snapped, the hall was at once filled with the noise of stamping feet, whistles and ironic cheers.

For a penny we would see a main picture, a cliffhanger serial and a comedy short with Chaplin, Buster Keaton, Larry Semon or the Keystone Cops. Though I think the comedies were the favourites with most of us, we loved the fights and stunts in the big picture: Rudolph Valentino fighting scores of men single-handed with his sword and leaping from a balcony to hang on a chandelier, men descending from aeroplanes on a rope to land on a train roof, Tom Mix leaping through an upper-storey window to land astride his wonderful white horse, Douglas Fairbanks fighting a ship-load of pirates unaided and never receiving a scratch. These were our heroes.

Dodging in without paying was discussed, and occasionally tried, but it rarely succeeded: all the tricks such as having an accomplice to open an emergency door from the inside were well known to the management. Once though, I did assist in a successful attempt. I was passing a cinema about the time of the early evening performance when a lad standing near the entrance said 'Hi kidda, want to dodge in?' I was interested. He explained his plot to me: we were to creep past the pay box where the lady was occupied with her knitting, and crouch just outside the inner doors until a paying customer passed through. Then we would creep in while the checkie was showing the customer to his seat. It sounded like a good plan. He warned me there was an iron post not far from the door and I would have to feel for it in the dark. 'Ye gan first,' he said. We crept past the pay box successfully and along the passage to the inner door. A customer passed in, and, when I judged it safe, I crept through the swing-door into the blackness beyond. I could hear the piano playing, but could see nothing. I moved forward a little and put out my hand to feel for the iron post. The iron post was wearing trousers. Suddenly a torch flashed down at me, a hand grabbed my jersey collar and yanked me to my feet. The checkie ran me along the passage and hurtled me into the street. I waited near the entrance, expecting at any moment to see my new found friend flying through the air as I had done, like a shovelful of coal, but nothing happened and it dawned on me that I had been tricked. He had sneaked in safely whilst I was being thrown out. He was a smart lad.

Near the bottom of the High Street and the cinema from which I had been forcibly ejected stood a picture house. This cinema bore the magnificent name of The Empress, but everyone called it 'Loppy Lloyds'. Lops was the local word for lice or fleas. We lads all believed it was possible to get into Loppy Lloyds by paying with two jam jars, yet none of us knew anyone who had actually tried to do so. One of the standing jokes of the time was that a stranger had proffered a pound note at the box office and had received his change in jam jars.

Sometimes, having no penny for the Scrush, my pal Richie and I would walk to Newcastle across the Swing Bridge in search of free entertainment and to enjoy the sounds and sights of a large city. We were two boys in much-darned jerseys and patched baggy shorts standing with our foreheads against the glass of shop windows, gazing with wistful admiration at the lavish displays inside: the pyramids of fruit and mounds of nuts in the fruiterer's; the richly decorated cakes; pork pies cut open to reveal boiled eggs; and pastries in the baker's; the profusion of sweets and chocolate bars displayed in neat patterns in the confectioner's.

We looked with fascinated horror at the legless ex-serviceman who used to propel himself along on a low trolley. The stumps of his thighs rested on leather pads and he used his hands and arms rather like a man rowing a boat. This sight branded itself into my memory. His method of begging was very simple – he parked in front of a house until given money to move on.

Whenever I hear the tune *Roses of Picardy*, I have an instant picture of the ex-servicemen's bands who used to play in the gutter in Northumberland Street – men with their medals pinned to their shabby raincoats and wearing flat caps and mufflers. Music was

such a rare treat in our lives that we would follow them round for a while when they changed pitches.

We took great delight in watching and listening to the buskers who performed for the queue waiting to enter the Theatre Royal – paper tearers, dancers, acrobats, musicians and magicians. We enjoyed them all.

This entertainment over, we would roam about to look at the stills in the foyers of cinemas and the gaudy posters and photographs of performers displayed in the entrances of the variety halls, the Empire, Palace and Hippodrome. None of the artists' names meant anything to us then, though many must have been names now legendary. I would like to have seen them.

On our visits to Newcastle we always ended up in the Bigg Market, which on Saturday afternoons was full of noise and bustle and a feeling of exuberant life: cheapjacks with croaky voices who attracted crowds and made them laugh with jokes we did not understand, quacks selling medicines, loud-voiced barrow boys shouting out prices. We were sometimes able to pick up a bruised apple or orange from under the barrow. Icecream sellers with Italian names sold sandwiches of enormous thickness for a penny. A hunchbacked strong man who bent iron bars about his neck fascinated us. Men with sandwich boards announcing that, 'The wages of Sin is Death' moved among the crowd and handed out tracts, and various speakers standing on boxes harangued any audience they could collect. By the time the flashing advert in coloured lights for Bovril was switched on, it was time for us to begin our long weary walk back to Windy Nook.

My pals and I belonged to no organisations – no Scouts, Boys' Brigade or clubs of any kind. The streets and plots of vacant land were our playgrounds. As boys usually do, we formed ourselves into small gangs. Each gang had a clearly recognisable call we used to contact each other. Ours sounded like 'Alley-oo-can'. Gangs often joined together to play our favourite games.

At times we used to lurk at the bottom of Sodhouse Bank, like Indians about to ambush a stage coach, and dash out to steal rides on the tram cars lumbering up the hill. We rode perched on the bumper, or crouched on the boarding step while hanging on to the handrail. The double-decker trams were roofless at the ends of the top deck and a conductor could see us by peering over the rails. Some ignored us, but others descended the stairs, took off the leather shoulder strap of their ticket machine, and swiped the backs and shoulders of the free riders to dislodge them; this added further zest to the game. After stopping at the Traveller's Rest public house at the top of the bank, the tram gathered speed and most of us did not risk any further, but one or two more daring ones did. One particular boy I remember used to sit on the boarding step with his legs outstretched and waving his hand in a devil-may-care way to anyone he saw. He was greatly admired for his dangerous feat.

One very odd pastime was popular for a while; this consisted of making what was called 'bangers' from a hollow key and a nail that fitted snugly into the hollow part of the key. We tied one end of a piece of string to the handle of the key and the other on to the nail near its head; a pinch of gunpowder was put into the hollow key and the nail inserted. This contraption was then swung, hard nail head first, against a stone or brick wall to cause a loud explosion. Boys bought the materials to make the gunpowder at chemists' shops and carried little tins of it in their pockets. They would offer a friend a pinch like a gentleman offering his snuffbox. I had a key and nail banger but never made any gunpowder; I relied on others to give me some. I recall that sometimes the hollow key would split with the explosion and it is amazing that no one ever blew off part of a finger or received any injury. Many of the corner stones of buildings were pock-marked with our bangers.

Boys of my age lived in a masculine world: apart from female relatives we hardly ever even spoke to a girl. All our games and pranks were for boys. Girls had their own games – Hitchy Dabber, skipping, playing at houses and making swings with doubled skipping ropes tied to the cross bar of a lamp post so they could sit on the end and twirl and untwirl around it. The only girls I remember being mentioned were the girls who worked at the rope factory and were known as 'Haggies Angels'. These girls were part of the mythology of the time and, listening to the curious tales told about them, I was glad I never encountered any of these dangerous damsels.

There was, however, an exception for me; this was Richie's sister Jenny. I harboured a secret affection for her. She attended the Central School and wore a navy blue gym slip, a blazer and a panama hat which she sometimes wore on the back of her head with the elastic round her neck. She used a school satchel with two leather straps going over her shoulders. She used to ruffle my hair and call me 'Dinger'. Her features were well formed and she had hazel eyes that always sparkled with laughter. I usually saw her when I was hanging about waiting for my pal to come out and she was coming home from school. We would chat for a while and she would tell me about her school. Once when I was looking at the marks made by her elastic garters when she was pulling up the black stockings on her skinny legs, she said to me, 'Gentlemen don't look at a lady's legs when she is pulling up her stockings.' She gave me a playful clout over the back of the head. I became aware for the first time that girls regarded their legs in a different way, not just as a means of walking.

One Saturday afternoon when I thought she was alone in the house, she played a trick on me. I saw her standing in the doorway. She had a toffee in her hand and held it up in a tempting sort of way and said, 'Would you like a toffee, Dinger?' and invited me into the house. I followed her in. She kept on changing the toffee from hand to hand as I reached out for it and then put both hands behind her back. I put both of my arms around her waist in an attempt to take the toffee from her. To my astonishment she said, 'Give me a kiss.' No sooner had my mouth touched hers than I leapt back as if her lips were red hot. I heard the sound of muffled giggling from the slightly open door of the cupboard under the stairs. Jenny opened the door angrily and the girls hiding there now laughed at the tops of their voices. I realised I had been the victim of a little plot and ran out of the house. I didn't even get my toffee. I vowed to myself I would never speak to Jenny again, but in time we became friends once more.

Shortly after being the victim of Jenny's prank, I obtained an early morning job with a farmer at Deckham who had just begun delivering milk in bottles. My job was to carry the bottles to the doorsteps and pick up the empties. My wage was two shillings and sixpence a week and a bottle of milk each day. I thought I was very well paid. On Saturday mornings and school holidays I was able to go back to the farm with the milk float and sometimes I was allowed to hold the reins for a while. I felt very important. I gave Mother the half-crown and she gave me sixpence for myself.

I envisaged a rich future with sixpence a week to spend, but my life pattern was about to change completely. One day when I came home from school, Mother told me we were going to move house again. This time we were going to the country to live in a place called Swinhope, in a cottage which cost two shillings and sixpence a week to rent. The year was 1925 and I was nearing my tenth birthday.

Swinhope

All our worldly goods had been loaded on the small flat lorry and my cousin, Tom Newton, and myself were perched on top of them. I sat in a kind of nest in Mother's feather bed and Tom sat in the shabby American rocking chair. Mother sat in the cab beside the driver with my young brother Norman on her knee. We left Gateshead early in the morning for Swinhope in Northumberland, about forty miles away. To us this seemed an enormous distance. I was filled with excitement at making a journey on a motor lorry, going to a new home and very happy because I was sharing the adventure with Tom whom I admired more than anyone I knew. We were very fortunate that the day was fine. It was one of those lovely days of summer when the whole world seems to sparkle and sing. Tom had brought his banjo and played and sang our favourite songs. I joined in the choruses with great delight – *Paddy McGinty's Goat, Felix Kept on Walking, Ivan Skavinsky Skavar.* I loved the last line of *Paddy McGinty's Goat* – 'The angel with the whiskers on was Paddy McGinty's goat', and we bawled it out with great glee, astounding village people who stood and gaped. We were amused at the effect and tried to sing louder.

I had only vague memories of visiting Swinhope with my Bell grandparents during the 1914-18 war, when I was a toddler. I remembered the journey to Allendale by train, and Jack Reed the elder, of Hope Head farm, meeting the tiny bus at Sparty Lea with a pony and trap. I could recall very clearly the feeling of jolting about on the rough limestone roads and one occasion when Jack's daughter Elsie took me for a walk through tall grass in the meadows where the feathery tops of the grass tickled my chin. I could also bring to mind the fun I experienced taking belly-flopper

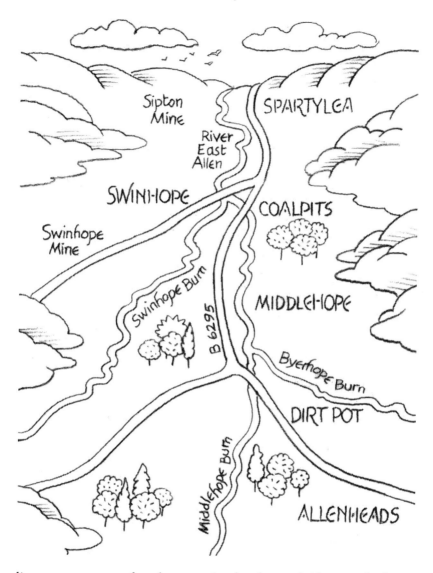

dives onto a mass of rushes growing by the roadside outside the cottage.

The tiny lorry groaned its way up the steep and winding road to the fell-top. Sometimes we had to cling to the tie ropes while going round sharp corners and we shouted with mock fear. Once on top we were in a new world. There was a fresher wind carrying strange and wonderful smells. The larks were singing joyously and appeared like black dots overhead and the peewits whirled and dived with frantic screams. We could hear the plaintive cries of the curlews and the sounds of other moorland birds. The noise of the lorry disturbed grouse among the ling at the roadside and they swished into the air as if hurled from a catapult with startled cries of 'g'back g'back'.

It must have been an emotional wrench for Mother to leave the town where she had always lived and where her brother and his family lived, to go to an isolated place where she knew no one, but she never complained or voiced any regret. Boy-like, I did not give my mother's feelings any thought. I was filled with the excitement of the journey, a new home, and the fresh sights and sounds.

At last, after what seemed to me an immense distance, and a great amount of rattling of furniture and bouncing about in my feather bed nest, we arrived in front of the cottage. It was tucked into a steep hillside a few yards from the road, and was built of millstone with a stone-flagged roof which, at the back, sloped down to within a foot of the ground. The flags were covered with green moss and houseleeks grew on the corners. We carried in our furniture and opened the windows to let in the air and sunshine. A gentle breeze puffed out the lace curtains like the sails of a ship. We dragged out the old, mouldy-smelling clippy mats from the stone floor and hung them to dry over the wooden railing surmounting the low stone wall around the front garden. The whole place smelled of damp stone, plaster and wet wallpaper which hung off the walls in places like melancholy flags. The fireplace was rusty and the grate full of damp soot. Mother lit a primus stove and we all enjoyed tea and corned beef sandwiches.

After tea, Ralph, the lorry driver, shook hands with Mother and said, 'God bless you Ada,' and climbed into the cab of his little lorry. Cousin Tom with his beloved banjo under his arm jumped in beside him and shouted 'Goodbye!' Tom kept on waving as the lorry sank out of sight on the steep hill near the cottage. We could still see him waving as the lorry reappeared on the little road. We watched and waved until all we could see was a tiny cloud of dust. I never saw Tom again. By the time I next visited my uncle and aunt in Gateshead, he had joined the army. He was captured at Dunkirk and died on the day of his release from the POW camp in a lorry accident in 1945.

We set to work to tidy up. To my great delight and wonder there was a wall bed in the corner where Norman and I were to sleep. The bed was folded up into a cupboard during the day and let down at night. We hauled out the mattress to air it beside the clippy mats, then stowed away the dishes, pots and pans and black lead brushes. Baking tins and cutlery were stored in the cupboard by the fireplace. I lit the fire with dry paper and sticks that Mother had thoughtfully brought with her and she began to prepare our evening meal while Norman and I explored the back garden. We devoured the small sour gooseberries, and tried the taste of the unripe blackcurrants growing amidst the nettles and docks. There was a mountain ash and an elm tree to climb. We ran up the mossy flagstones of the roof at the back and sat astride the coping stones where we could see almost the whole of Swinhope, a little dale about a mile and a half in length running roughly east to west with its high western end stopped by Killhope Law, crowned by its boundary cairn. I was told later that it was possible to stand in three counties at once on Killhope top; Northumberland, Durham and Cumberland and on fine days you could see Yorkshire as well.

Next day work started in earnest. Mother told us to scrub the sandstone floor which, when newly cleaned, showed the grain like freshly-planed wood. We then scraped the rust from the fireplace and black-leaded it with Zebo grate polish. After burnishing the rusty steel fender with emery paper, we finished it off with Brasso, whitewashed the hearth and polished the brass handle of the oven and the tap of the boiler at the side of the fire. Fortunately the lovely weather continued and the cottage began to dry out. We had our first experience of those lovely days which occur in Pennines country. I should have been going to school, but Mother decided it was not worth while my starting so close to the holidays and I was free, apart from household chores, to roam about exploring to my heart's content. I rejoiced in my freedom. It was during these days I learned to love the fells and dales of Northumberland. I know of no other countryside that has the same magic and beauty or gives the same sense of freedom. I walked with high steps among the ling and heather, splashed through the bogs where the rushes grew and where there were bright green patches of sphagnum moss, speckled in places with small spots of crimson. I scrambled among the outcrops of millstone grit and drank from cool springs and sometimes from the little burns tumbling down worn clefts where the bracken grew higher than my head. I crawled among the bracken and enjoyed the shade and its pungent smell. I imagined myself like Crusoe on an island. On the higher ridges I delighted in the cool breeze on my face. The cries of the birds and the bleating of the sheep enhanced my feeling of solitude. From the high ridges I could see the farmhouses in unknown dales revealed by the scarves of smoke from their chimneys.

At times I wandered by the burnside and returned again and again to a favourite haunt, a long stretch of slow, still water about five feet deep, where the drooping branches of the willows growing on both sides of the burn intermingled with each other to form a tunnel. I swam here frequently, exulting in the velvety feel of the water and the smell of the willows, the burn and the meadowsweet growing on the bankside. A sweet secret place this, where after my swim I would lie on my back to dry in the sun. Everything was fresh and new to me. Dragonflies frequented the burnside. They flew erratically and would pause almost motionless for a brief moment before resuming their swift zig-zagging course. There were three kinds – a small blue one, a much larger pale green kind and a rarer sort coloured like a wasp. Bees buzzed around – the common bumble bee with black and yellow stripes, the fat gingery ones looking like blobs of marmalade zooming about, and the black ones with the red behinds which seemed as if each had been daubed with a paintbrush as it left the nest. I took great pleasure in watching the brilliant butterflies landing and shuddering on the flowers. My favourite was a bright blue about the size of a little fingernail, which seemed never to land anywhere and was always searching.

As I lay there in the sun I heard occasionally the skirr skirr sound of a whetstone on a scythe blade, the whirring noise of the mowing machine with its click click at the corner of the set, sometimes, as if from many miles away, a faint human voice or a dog's bark. At times I was startled by a sandpiper's explosive dash through the willow tunnel. I shared what I thought of as my own secret place with little speckled lizards with pop eyes which came out of their hiding places to bask on the sun-warmed stones on the bank, the cruising trout in the burn and the wagtails dancing on the large burn stones.

Not far from my willow tunnel, at the foot of a meadow slanting down to the burnside, there was a huge boggy patch where masses of creamy double buttercups grew. I used to gather bunches of them to take home for Mother. A few years later someone drained the field and they all died. So much beauty destroyed for a few pennyworths of hay.

Each day began with one of us on our knees, as if in prayer, cleaning out the cinders and ashes of the old fire and lighting a new one. As the fire burned and crackled into life, Mother boiled a kettle on the primus stove to make tea. The fire was the hub of our lives, necessary for warmth, cooking, hot water and our daily bread, but it was a tyrant. I was always looking for wood for kindling and oven heating. Even paper was scarce as we were unable to buy newspapers or magazines. Every piece of wrapping paper or cardboard box was carefully hoarded in the cupboards near the fire. The ancient Victorian oven required enormous amounts of fuel to reach baking heat and was very sulky, sometimes needing as much fuel as would have supplied a head of steam for a river steamer. Mother used to judge its heat by holding the brass ring of its handle; she would click her tongue sadly and say, 'That dratted oven.' This usually happened on baking days. The bread tins would be in a line on the fender for the dough to rise; the fork-pricked dough gave me the impression of a line of babies in cradles. When the oven was slow to heat I would have to set off and look for fuel. Sometimes in desperation I would take a sack and gather ling to feed the oven. 'Like feeding an elephant with sponge cake,' Mother would say, but the ling burned fiercely while it lasted and brought up the temperature to baking heat. Then the house would be filled with the lovely smell of baking bread.

One day Norman had a bright idea: when rummaging round in a disused quarry where people dumped rubbish he found some old bicycle tyres. We chopped them into pieces and fed them to the oven. The result was spectacular. There was a sort of damped explosion, a great roaring sound, and with a tremendous whoosh the chimney caught fire. We rushed out to watch. The top of the chimney was like a huge Roman candle scattering sparks and red-hot pieces of soot for miles around.

I searched for oven-heating wood and kindling as diligently as a prospector seeking precious ore. I hauled driftwood from the burn and left it on the bank to dry in the sun. I climbed trees to break off dead branches and when I could not reach them, threw up a clothes line with a stone tied on the end to haul the branches down.

Not far away from our cottage there was an uninhabited house falling into ruin. The windows were all out and, where the rain had blown in, the wooden floor upstairs had rotted in places and part of the staircase had also crumbled away; otherwise the house was intact. Even the front door on its rusty hinges was still there. Later, someone told me that the man who had lived there many years ago had one day walked away and never returned. No one knew what had happened to him. By the time we arrived in Swinhope no one could even remember his name for sure, but one person did say he thought his name was Fattle. My imagination prompted me to invent a reason for his disappearance. I saw him as a big man with a fat face walking down the road, wearing a bowler hat and an overcoat, going off to join the army. The walls of this house had never been papered but had been decorated with red ochre wash which was now very faint. I examined the walls very carefully hoping to find a scrawled message or at least a name, but there was nothing. All I found among the damp, fallen plaster on the ground was a bone-handled pocketknife with a broken blade.

I began by taking pantry shelves and windowsills. These were made of a straight grained wood, just right for splitting into kindling. Mother was worried at first about this pillaging of a deserted house, wondering if it was theft, but I comforted myself by reasoning that since the owner had abandoned the house, it belonged to no one. For a while I had a slight fear that the owner might return and find me demolishing his house, but this faded in time. To us it really was a treasure house, providing precious kindling and oven-heating baulks on baking days for a long time. Eventually we burnt all the wood in the house.

Mother wrote to my Aunt Dora asking her to send us old newspapers and magazines for the fire lighting. For a few days we had a feast of reading *Titbits, Answers, Everybody's Weekly,* and *John Bull.* When we had read and re-read the magazines, Mother gleaned a second harvest by searching for offers of free samples and catalogues. Sending for catalogues ensured the postman's calling and he would collect letters to post. Mother enjoyed browsing and admiring the illustrations of ladies' wear, while Norman and I spent much time looking through a huge catalogue from May's of Birmingham which sold everything. I used to read all the descriptions of the bicycles and tools with interest, comparing racing and roadster models and admiring bikes with translucent tyres and back-pedalling brakes. Finally the catalogues served as firelighters. Mother sent for all free samples offered. We received tiny tins of Gibbs Dentifrice about the size of a shilling, little tubes of Euthymol toothpaste about the size of a little finger, cures for corns, piles, ointments, chocolate flavoured laxatives, Tokalon face powder, vanishing cream, and minute boxes of pills and various little bottles of patent medicines which claimed to cure most ailments.

Mr J.V. Hill kept a small general dealer's shop in Allenheads, about two miles away. He rode round on a pony once a month to collect orders. He sold paraffin oil, clog bottoms for re-soling clogs or turning old boots into clogs, clog irons, hardware, haberdashery and always had a suitcase with samples of shirts and various ladies' garments. He loved a joke and when he laughed his

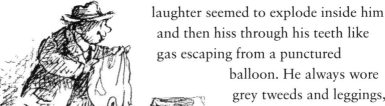

laughter seemed to explode inside him and then hiss through his teeth like gas escaping from a punctured balloon. He always wore grey tweeds and leggings, a celluloid collar with rounded corners, a black bootlace tie and a wide-brimmed trilby hat. He looked exactly right for playing the part of a bank manager in a western film.

'Now Ada,' he would say, holding up a pair of fleecy lined bloomers, 'that's a fine knicker!' We would all collapse with laughter. Mother would hold her left side and curl over as she did when overcome with laughter and J.V. Hill would hiss out some more laughing gas.

Our coal was delivered by the ton load; it had to be ordered well in advance and cost about twenty-one shillings a ton. We had a very lean time when the coal was bought. Poor Mother had to spend most of a week's income on coal and somehow feed us at the same time. She always managed and we were never starved, though in the lean times, when coal had to be bought and when the quarter's rent had to be paid, we were very close to it. During these hard times we lived chiefly on porridge, bread, vegetable pancakes sometimes flavoured with a morsel of cheese or a little piece of bacon, and we always had eggs. At least we were never short of bread as so many people were at that time, particularly in 1926.

Allendale Cooperative Wholesale Society sent round a traveller once a month to collect orders for groceries. They were delivered by cart from Allendale. When the snow was deep they were delivered the by a horse-drawn sledge. It was often dark before they arrived in Swinhope and from our doorway we would be able to see the light of the hurricane lamp on the sledge, dipping and reappearing like the light of a small boat in a rough sea, as the horse ploughed its way through the snow drifts. This delivery service was our lifeline. Thirl, the deliveryman had a very tough job having to make his way to every house. In fine weather he could leave the cardboard box of groceries at an agreed place; the packages were perfectly safe, as no one would touch them.

We boys looked forward to delivery day as the cardboard box of groceries always contained our monthly treat of sweets, frequently a packet of the black minty sweets we called black bullets. If I was over eager and tried to get at the sweets before Mother had checked the contents with her list, she would pick up the wet dishcloth and give me a token swipe with it.

Mother ordered her flour, feeding stuffs for the hens' crowdy, bran, boxings and Indian meal, from Allendale millers who also sent round a traveller and delivered orders.

I sought milk daily from the farm of Mary and Joe Burton. I paid for a pint, received a quart and, in addition, Mary frequently gave me a little gift such as a piece of gingerbread or some biscuits, and on her baking days a couple of scones or a tea cake. Mary had a strange appearance because of some accident, which had left her with a permanently twisted neck, and she had to turn her whole head to look at anyone, rather as a hen does. She would come out of the dairy with my quart can filled to the brim and my gift wrapped in a piece of butter paper. She would hold out the can and the package and say, 'Put this in th'pocket lad.' I think she had the sweetest nature and kindest heart of anyone I have ever known. Joe, her husband, had been gassed during the war, and was an invalid, unable to do much work. They had no children. I always admired her beautiful kitchen, spotless and shining, and was fascinated by the china ornaments of cows and horses on the mantelpiece. Her brightly coloured clippy mats felt luxurious underfoot and looked as if they had just been made and put down that morning.

One fine day we saw Joe make a bonfire in the garden and burn all his army clothing, except his puttees which he gave to me. I did not understand then why he should do this. I only saw a splendid army greatcoat going up in flames; I felt a sense of loss and wished he had given it to me.

In retrospect I am amazed that Mother adapted so well to a completely new pattern of life; adjusted to once a month delivery of groceries, paraffin lighting, seeking water from a well that sometimes froze, cooking in a primitive oven, on the fire and occasionally on a primus stove. She had to rely on J.V. Hill and postal orders for clothing and in the earliest days she knew no one and lived among people whose speech was, at times, quite incomprehensible to her.

Allendonian speech was roughly like the language of the Authorised Version of the Bible, but the phrases had worn smooth through time as had the polished stones in the burn. Phrases like 'hearest thou', 'seest thou', 'couldest thou' had become 'heest-ta', 'seest-ta' and 'coulds-th' and so on. Some phrases could be learned only in usage, rather like learning a tune. A common expletive was 'Gar bon'. It must, I think, have been originally a French phrase which had drifted south from Scotland at a time when French was a strong influence there. Some words were archaic and had dropped out of general use centuries previously; one example was the use of the word jealous meaning to be suspicious. We boys, as youngsters do, soon picked up the dialect mixing with our friends at school, but Mother took some time to understand local speech and never used it herself.

Gradually we became familiar with and made many friends among the people of Swinhope and were accepted, as far as incomers (as people from other places were known) ever could be. Mother began attending the Methodist Chapel and found companionship there, while Norman and I made pals at school and through time got to know neighbouring farmers.

One day as I sat by the burnside I could hear people behind me, on the other side of the dyke, working in the meadow. They were turning the swathes of scythe-mown grass on the steep part of the meadow where the mowing machine could not be used. I turned my head to look at them, but I was too shy to speak and make myself known. A man about forty years of age, wearing shabby trousers, an unfastened waistcoat over a union shirt and a straw hat, shouted, 'Woulds't th' like to help with the hay lad?' I jumped over the dyke and he gave me a rake to join them in swathe turning. He was Joe Parker Reed and he and his family befriended me when I needed it most. I felt quite pleased with myself being accepted and having a job to do, and later in the day, when the rows of hay were swept into heaps for pike making and Joe Parker asked me to ride the horse while he held the sweep, I was filled with delight. I told Mother very proudly that I was working and that I would have to be up early in the morning to help with the harvest.

Mother's Swinhope days were the happiest period of her life. A few months after we first arrived she was very ill and the doctor said she would die. Thank God she did not. After recovering, apart from a cough that plagued her throughout her life, she had no more severe health problems. She adapted to country life remarkably well, made very firm friendships and was a wonderful mother to us two boys.

One of her kind friends gave her a matting frame and she learned how to make proggy and hooky mats. People used to gather in each other's houses during the dark nights to help make mats. The burlap was stretched out and fastened on the frame which rested on a couple of chair backs and could be adjusted as the mat progressed. People sat round facing each other as they worked so they could enjoy a bit of gossip or jokes and tales of former times as they progged or hooked in the cloth. They made proggy mats by sticking in little pieces of cloth about two inches long with a little spike; and the hooky kind by weaving a long strip in and out of the burlap with a hooked tool. They worked to a design drawn on the burlap backing with a puce pencil, a copying ink pencil, and some times they used both the hooky and the proggy method to form a contrast.

These matting parties provided great enjoyment; the hostess cleaned the lamp glass and trimmed the wicks of the oil lamp ready for the occasion, and baked scones, buns and biscuits for refreshment. The balls of matting cloths and clippy pieces, made from old garments and dyed when required, were placed in readiness. As the ladies worked they nattered and joked. They wove in stories, tales and bits of scandal with the fabric, and, as they poked holes in the cloth, they poked holes in the reputation of the staunch chapel folk whose conduct had not always been of high moral standard.

At times the ladies leaned their heads together and kept their voices low to relate things we boys had not to hear. I would just catch cryptic little snippets which I did not quite understand: 'I think she's been behind the dyke again.' 'Hardly him, he's old enough to be her father.' 'Her grandfather, more like.' They all enjoyed a laugh. 'I think I've got a bit of your old bloomers here, Ada,' someone would say, holding up a piece of cloth; more laughter. Refreshments over, a lady named Mrs Milburn always said, 'Come on now Norman, give us a concert.'

Norman had a very clever gift of mimicry, and for the entertainment of the matting party would perform mimes, little comic episodes already well-known to the company. One was of

an enormously fat lady accompanied by two
young girls who had come to Swinhope
for a holiday and was
attempting to mount a
stile. She had had
several attempts, one
girl standing on top of
the stile to pull her up
and the other
shoving with her
shoulder under the
enormous backside.

Norman put on a pinny and a hat of Mother's and mimed the
event, using a chair as the stile and being each of the characters in
turn. Next he would mime a local man who had stayed too long in
the beer tent on a show day and, while staggering home, found it
impossible to go any further and had draped himself over a dyke
like a piece of washing to dry.

One of Norman's most popular turns concerned a local
woman who, not wanting her husband to go out without her, had
dug a hole in the garden and buried all his best clothes to prevent
his going. Mother's laughter bubbled up like a spring and she had
to hold her left side and the tears came into her eyes. Mother's
matting parties were always popular; they were the only ones with
a cabaret as well as gossip and refreshments.

The party over, the guests set off for home. As soon as the
door opened the wind gusted in making the flames of the paraffin
lamp leap up the glass chimney and leave sooty marks inside. One
of the ladies in a black cape, holding an old-fashioned candle
lamp, looked as if she had strayed from a novel by Mrs Gaskell.

The matting parties provided a very welcome diversion during
the long evenings when we rarely saw anyone. We were all avid

readers, but had no source of books. Then about two years after I left school, a little library, funded by the Scottish philanthropist Andrew Carnegie, opened for the public at the school. Mother said, 'There is corn in Egypt.' I have always been grateful to Mr Carnegie.

The little library was replenished monthly, I think; Norman brought home three books at a time. Some of my favourite authors turned up: William le Queux, Sapper and John Buchan, but among the lucky dip of books I also made some new discoveries. The most influential of these was *Huckleberry Finn*. It ranked in importance in my mind with my discovery of *Robinson Crusoe* in Gateshead Library. Mark Twain's sense of humour is, at times, very like a Northumbrian's – oblique and sardonic. Many years later I read in a magazine that he was in fact, on his Mother's side, descended from a well-known Northumbrian family.

I enjoyed H.G. Wells. I remember reading *Kipps* and *Love and Mr Lewisham* in which I found out about Mr Lewisham studying from books and making a timetable for different subjects. I was astounded by this simple and obvious fact. The thought excited me but I had no access to books for study and several years passed before I did anything about it. Strangely, it never entered my mind to seek advice or help anywhere. But the seed was there.

Before the opening of the library, Mother's reading was restricted to her Bible and paperback novels of E.M. Dell, Annie S. Swan, Ruby M. Ayres and Sheila K. Smith, mostly given to her by Aunt Dora or some summer visitor.

Mother was quite unaware that some of the books she enjoyed were classics. She discovered authors who were to become her favourites: Thomas Hardy, Mrs Gaskell, the Brontës, George Elliot and Nathaniel Hawthorne. It is easy to understand why she could identify so easily with Hardy and his tragic heroines and with Jane Eyre. My own love for Thomas Hardy came many years later.

With a book to read by the fire, and a potato or an onion baking in the oven for supper, we were happy and content.

In summer we looked forward very much to visits by my Aunt Dora and my cousins Olive, Winnie and Jenny. It was a great joy for us to have someone different to talk to. They brought us bundles of magazines and we shared with them the stocks of tinned food they provided – tins of fruit, salmon, and tongue, great luxuries to us. Aunt Dora and Mother talked and talked.

From our visitors, we received news of the outside world; of the new Tyne Bridge and the latest marvel, talking pictures. My cousins taught us the latest popular songs. My pal, Bill Philipson would join us and we sang these as we climbed Killhope for a picnic or lay drying in the sun after swimming in Swinhope dam. Our voices went echoing about the lonely places making the sheep stare curiously before they fled and the birds take to the air as they heard *Tiptoe through the Tulips, I'm Painting the Clouds with Sunshine*, 'Have You Ever Been Lonely, Have You Ever Been Blue?'

Our high spirits induced us to run, trying to keep up with wind-blown clouds and jump about on wobbly shog-bogs until they burst. Shog-bogs were like huge green balloons where water, unable to drain away, had forced the turf to bloat upwards. When they burst, the water spouted upwards as if from a whale.

In season we gathered bilberries in the woods at Allenheads to make gorgeous pies and tarts, and collected rosehips for Mother to make jelly. None of us even knew the word vitamin in those days and Mother was very pleased to find out years later how valuable to health they were.

These summer days passed all too quickly and when visitors departed it was rather an anticlimax. We would walk with them to the bus stop at Sparty Lea and the cottage seemed rather desolate to us for a few days.

A Country School

As soon as I stepped through the gateway into the boys'
yard of St Peter's School I was grabbed by a big lad in
corduroy knickerbockers, a striped shirt and a floppy
peaked cap hanging over one side of his head. 'Let's wrastle,' he
said, and facing me with his hands on my shoulders told me to do
the same. He immediately began kicking at my ankles to bring me
down. His clogs raised clouds of dust and sent small stones flying.
I jumped and hopped about avoiding his kicks. I had two
advantages; I was much more agile and wearing shoes helped my
movements. I concentrated on defensive tactics. I was aware of a
blur of faces of those watching and could hear the mingled shouts,
yells and laughter and some shriller sounds from the girls leaning
over the wall that separated the two yards. At last I sensed one of
his swinging kicks, hooked my foot behind his ankle and brought
him down with a thump. I stood beside him, prepared to run if he
sought revenge some other way; but I was saved this indignity by
the tolling of the school bell in the little tower at one end of the
roof.

We all shuffled into the schoolroom, some kicking stones,
others playing a last minute game of tiggy. I paused and looked
about me at this lovely September morning and caught a glimpse
of a passing carter sitting on the front of his cart with a pipe in his
mouth. I envied him.

The school was one large room with a little annex for the
infants who were taught by Miss Stokoe, the Head Master's only
assistant. The Head had to cope alone with all the classes from
standard one onwards.

The high windows of the gaunt classroom were mostly on the
eastern wall and hardly any sunshine came in. We sat in groups of

four at heavy oak desks with cast iron ends. The walls were painted a dirty cream and were devoid of decoration apart from a large map of the world with the British Empire in red, and a picture of Jesus with a flaxen beard.

The first morning back from the holiday there was a strong smell of soap and disinfectant mingling with the farm smell of clothing and the old wooden desks. The wall facing us as we sat at our desks was a blind wall without windows but had a door leading through to the infants' room. Near this wall there was a huge cast-iron stove surrounded by a strong wire mesh fireguard with a brass rim. The Head's big kneehole desk stood near the stove.

St Peter's School served an area for miles around ranging from the farms on the very edge of the fell on Killhope side to the top end of Swinhope at Hope Head and down to the farms at Tedham Green and Sipton.

In times of heavy snowstorms many of the children were snowbound and enjoyed extra holidays at home while the senior boys joined in with the men cutting snow on the roads for seven shillings a day. Senior boys were also unofficially excused when the harvest was late and they had to help get in the hay during the last spell of fine weather in September. We left school at fourteen years of age, except for those like myself who were lucky enough to have a birthday during a holiday and could leave at thirteen, at the end of the term.

The school stood by the side of the little road which climbed and wound its way round Killhope to Nenthead and Alston in Cumberland and was surrounded by meadows and pastureland where the lads sometimes held Cumberland style wrestling matches.

My old foe, mental arithmetic was my first lesson. The subject was fraught with apprehension and unpleasant memories.

'A grocer buys sugar at so much per hundredweight and sells it at so much per pound. What is his profit per hundredweight?'

I had a very clear picture in my mind of a grocer in a white coat making up pound bags of sugar he had scooped out of a sack, but as I did not know how many pounds in a hundredweight and the sums of money mentioned had fled my memory, I had to use my old trick of bluffing, gazing into space and mumbling my lips as if making abstruse calculations.

The lad next to me nudged me and pointed to his slate. I was full of gratitude to this boy, whose name I found was Bill Philipson, and wrote down the answer. Working on slates had several advantages: it was easy to spit on the slate, rub out anything wrong with the cuff of jacket or jersey and write in the correct answer and as it was a clumsy business to collect them for marking, it was rarely done; so I continued with my deceit. All mental calculations were beyond me and I did not know any of the tables of weights and measures completely. What I did know merely confused me: why did a measure for liquids suddenly become a measure for peas and beans? Why measure distances in miles and furlongs then change over to chains, rods, poles and perches? Was a rood, I wondered, the same thing as a rod? Strangely it never entered my head to ask the master. To my great relief, 'Chappie', as the children had named the Head Master, seemed not to punish those unable to perform mental gymnastics.

How accurate children's nicknames for people usually are. Chappie was a small dapper man with his dark wavy hair brushed straight up. His appearance always reminded me of the picture in the comic strips of a man who has seen a ghost. He was always very neatly dressed in a light grey suit and was clean-shaven. He blinked almost incessantly, particularly when addressing pupils or asking a question. Perhaps this nervous habit was the result of the First World War in which he had served as a sergeant in an infantry regiment on the Western Front. I suppose this little country school was what he had dreamed about during the dreadful war years. At this time the school numbered about sixty pupils and not one left unable to read and write.

I admired Chappie because he had been a soldier and because he had a gold hunter watch which he kept in a little leather bag in his waistcoat pocket. Chappie drove to school in a little blue Clyno motor car with a canvas hood and a dicky seat. This gained him great esteem in our eyes, as it was the only car in the neighbourhood. Sometimes he chose two reliable pupils to go home with him to help in his garden. On these occasions we scrambled with each other to open the double gates in the girls' yard and stood in a bunch cheering as the car turned out into the road with one smirking lad in the dicky seat and the other beside Chappie who wore his gauntlets and tweed cap for driving. We all longed to be picked for this honour but I was never one of the lucky ones.

My greatest disappointment at this school was that there were almost no books apart from the readers and a few textbooks. When the depressing thought of going back to school again after the long freedom of summer had come to me I had hoped, as a consolation, that there might be some interesting books to read. There was I remember, a set of *The Young Fur Traders* and a few copies of *Mr Midshipman Easy* and *Westward Ho!* I'd read these books long before and to my disgust there was nothing new. There was however one grain of comfort; there were two volumes of Chappell's *Book of Knowledge* which Chappie permitted me to take home.

I read these through, skipping what did not interest me. I do not know if I remembered very much, but the article on Shakespeare made an indelible impression. It was I think the first time I'd come across his name. Included in the article was a picture of Autolycus accompanying the verses of his song and the *Winter Song* from *Love's Labour's Lost*. Apart from nursery rhymes this was my first acquaintance with poetry and it delighted me so much that I memorised both songs.

Poetry did not interest Chappie very much. I do not think there were any poetry anthologies in the school, but on one occasion he did read Kingsley's *The Knight's Leap at Altenahr* to us and set us on the task of memorising the verses written on the board.

On certain of the glorious days of spring and early summer Chappie would stand beside a window staring and blinking at the outside world. 'Now sit up straight', he'd say when he faced us. We were all eager obedience and elbowed in the side any sluggard and hissed 'Nature walk!'

'Ah now, Barbara and Elsie, I would like you to keep an eye on the juniors while we are outside.'

Poor Barbara and Elsie, the two oldest girls and the most trustworthy, had to suffer for being reliable and conscientious, unless they enjoyed their brief authority. The rest of us sat upright, hands behind our backs, models of obedience waiting to be unleashed.

Usually we walked up the Back Lonnen or along Swinhope Lonnen; we boys straggled behind, climbed over dykes into the pastures and playfully wrestled with each other or rolled on the ground in delight. The peewheets screeched at us, wove their patterns in the air, dived, just skimming our heads and making us cringe. The larks rose straight up as if being hauled to the sky by invisible wires. We teased the girls by chasing them with a slug on the end of a stick or made them shriek by pretending to put little green frogs from the ditches down the backs of their necks. The girls plucked the delicate blue and yellow pansies growing abundantly by the side of the road to make posies to fasten to their pinafores, and gathered long stemmed flowers to take back to school. I found the names of the flowers Chappie identified for us fascinating: Ragged Robin, Red Campion, Cowslip, Eyebright, and Stitchwort and remembered them effortlessly, but his little lectures on parts of the flowers and fertilisation did not interest me at the time and the information was quickly forgotten.

'There he is!' Bill shouted excitedly. 'Under that big stone in the middle!' I'd removed my shirt and I lay flat on the stone as I'd seen Bill do and began probing with my hands to find openings where the fish might be hiding. I could feel the warm sun on my back and I was breathing in the tangy smell of the burn with my face nearly in the water. I moved my hands very slowly as Bill had instructed me. At last my probing fingers found the belly of the fish. I was tingling with excitement and dreaded losing him now. I slowly got a grip of the body just below the head and could feel it trying to wriggle free. I withdrew my arm and there was a quick flashing arc in the sunlight as it landed on the burnside where Bill pounced on it and killed it. I was jubilant at my success.

We continued fishing for some time; we stamped on the bankside to frighten a fish from its lurking place underneath and then watched carefully where it sought refuge under a stone, Bill was an expert at this game and had taught me how to hand-fish for trout. He always caught many more than I did, but always shared the catch equally.

Our fishing over for the time being, we lay on our backs in the sun chewing a piece of grass, spitting green and watching the wagtails bobbing on the stones in the burn. A huge green dragonfly darted, hovered and zig zaggd over the burn. Our catch of lovely dappled trout with pink spots on their pearly grey undersides lay in a shady spot nearby. The only sound was the

guggling of the burn water flowing over the stones in shallow places.

'How do the blokes get to these places?' Bill asked.

'I think they get a job on a ship and then jump ship.' I replied.

'But how do they know where a ship's going to?'

I didn't know the answer to that question.

My cousin Tom had sent me some *Wide World* magazines from Gateshead and our imaginations had been fired with the romantic stories of pearl diving in the South Seas, lumber jacking in Canada, gold and diamond mining in South Africa, sheep farming in New Zealand and being a sailor on a square rigged ship.

I thought we'd try the South Seas first. The story we'd read about brown skinned girls who wore grass skirts and who swam naked in the sea was very appealing. We decided after discussion

that we'd do all these things in time, but that we'd begin in the
South Seas.

Then we noticed in the distance Shield's little bus looking no
bigger than a match box, slowly moving along the road on its
return journey from Allendale Station to Allenheads and realised
with a shock that it was late afternoon and that it was many hours
since we'd sneaked away from school at dinner time to play the
wag. We suddenly knew we were very hungry. We set off home
with our fish. I could see in anticipation Ma frying the trout in
oatmeal, I'd be able to say this time that I had caught some myself.
I turned for a moment and saw Bill, with his catch on a string in
his hand, moving swiftly over the ground with his tireless loping
run in the opposite direction towards Tedham Green.

Bill and I often played truant during that last year at school.
We were always caned the next morning, but we didn't mind much
and the fun was well worth the punishment. I thought the price
very cheap as Chappie's caning was very light compared to the
vicious swiping I'd experienced in Gateshead. Though Ma didn't
approve of my truanting it did not worry her very much. She
usually said, 'Mind they will put you in the bad boys' school.' In
Ma's mind all people in authority were lumped together in a
generalised 'they'.

On very warm days Bill and I found the burn irresistible, and
the thought of going back into school unbearable. Nearly always
we spent these stolen afternoons playing by the burnside and
'dooking'. When we found a deep pool scoured out by the winter
floods, we stripped off and set to work clearing out the rubbish
and large stones. We used these large stones with alternate layers
of turves from the bankside to make a wall across the burn and
add depth to the swimming hole. We would wade in the pool
about waist deep, feeling with our feet for large stones or rubbish
such as old bed ends, and plunge in to roll the stones away and

clear other obstacles before coming up for breath.

We swam naked and, to dry ourselves, ran up and down the burnside, our feet gilded with buttercup pollen. When dry, we sat in a sunny spot letting the sunshine warm us. When Bill had a fag cadged from his elder brothers, we shared it, passing it back and forth for a couple of draws each.

The four terms I spent at St Peter's were largely wasted. We senior boys were bored most of the time and we were mischievous to alleviate the boredom. There was no physical education of any kind, no organised games and no art, craft or science lessons. The only musical instrument in the school was Chappie's tuning fork. With this he performed wonders as I learned about eight songs while I was there. For music lessons the whole school sang together. It must have been a relief for him to deal with a single group instead of dashing from one group to another like one of those Chinese jugglers who spin plates on top of sticks. He began by tapping the note from his fork and asking us to hum the note. The various noises that came out were unbelievable, a weird assortment of sounds which made my pal Bill Philipson and me dissolve in helpless laughter. Apart from hymn singing in Chapel, there was no music in our lives at all and since many of the children did not even attend Chapel it was hardly surprising they could not hum a given note. Next, Chappie would hum a few bars and get us to join in. He progressed like this until we achieved the tune and words of a song. His tenacity and patience were outstanding and I've always been amazed that he achieved so much. I loved the singing lessons. These songs like, *The Farmer's Boy*, *The Minstrel Boy*, *The Vicar of Bray*, *The Mermaid*, and *Shenandoah*, and *Hearts of Oak*, were the only poetry and music in our lives and for me the only real enjoyment in school.

Bill Philipson and I were close pals throughout our time in school and for a long time afterwards. Through boredom and monotony we were often in trouble. Bill had a knack of making things funny and causing fits of giggling. Also he had a fund of stories, limericks and riddles learned from his elder brothers. We did many stupid things such as chewing pieces of blotting paper and sticking them on the ceiling by flicking them upwards with a ruler. Of course we flicked them at other pupils whenever Chappie's attention was elsewhere or when he went into the infants' room to have a chat with Miss Stokoe. When this happened a mini-snowstorm of missiles flew all over the classroom. We teased the girls in silly ways, such as tying their pinafore strings to the desk and stealing their hair ribbons. I used to pass messages to Mary Carruthers who had a round smiling face and beautiful hair done up in plaits that reached to her waist. I sent her messages attempting to arrange trysts, but these meetings never came off. She did permit me once to walk home with her, but as soon as she approached her house she ran off like a frightened deer.

Another of our misdemeanours was smoking in the lavatory, a smelly rectangle of concrete with walls covered in algae and a good crop of well-nourished moss resulting from competitions to see who could pee the highest. There was also a line of seats over a dank earth closet. A group of us used to gather at morning break and at dinner times for a smoke. I rarely had cigarettes but my pal Bill Philipson always shared with me.

'Where dids't th' get them?' Our eyes grew large and our mouths opened with astonishment when John Lee, whom we sometimes called 'Little Bogs' because his Father was known as 'Jack o' the Bogs', had nonchalantly produced a brown packet of twenty Full Strength Capstan and passed it around. To us a packet of five Woodbines was a luxury and twenty Capstan left us overawed and puzzled about the source. We all lit up and puffed, coughed and spluttered. The lavatory was like a kippering shed.

This plenitude continued for a while and then stopped abruptly. Eventually John Lee satisfied our curiosity and confessed that the cigarettes were stolen from a cupboard at home and had been, incredibly, bought for his Mother when she was ill! He told us the Doctor had ordered them. We all regretted the end of this bounty but John Whitfield, who was the most addicted to smoking, was very dismayed. John was an only child. He often plagued his mother with requests for money to buy cigarettes. Once when she refused, he grabbed a carving knife from the kitchen table and threatened to cut off a cow's tail if she didn't give him twopence for a packet of Woodbines. When his father returned from his shift at Sipton lead mine, and heard about John's threat, his temper exploded: he unbuckled his leather belt and chased John round the table swiping at him. John's mother took her husband's dinner and followed him round with it in her hand trying to pacify him by crying 'Come on love, get th' dinner.' Intent on punishment and exasperated by his wife's cries of, 'Get th' dinner love,' the father suddenly turned round and, giving a high kick like a chorus girl, kicked the plate from his wife's hands and the mince and dumplings spattered all over the ceiling. John fled.

We senior boys sat at the far end of the room at the back; we were furthest away from authority, but also furthest away from the stove. During the bitterly cold days we were too dispirited even to get into mischief. The stove would be stoked up to its maximum heat, with part of its iron chimney glowing red, but only a few yards away the cold was almost unbearable; we could hardly hold a pen or slate pencil and had to do exercises such as astride jumping and thigh slapping to warm up.

Near the door the softer wood of the floor had been worn away by generations of iron-shod clogs leaving the hard knots in the wood like little black mushrooms. Moaning icy winds swept the porch and hurtled under the door to swallow up heat from the

stove and freeze our feet and legs. When it snowed, eddies of snow blew under the door and danced their way as far as the warm space in front of the stove. We all hoped it would snow hard enough to block up the roads then we could stay off school and join the snow cutters.

On the frequent wet days we were allowed to drape our soaked jackets and coats over the fireguard. As the clothes steamed, smells of byres and barns, stables and sheepfolds were released and spread throughout the bleak classroom like a kind of earthy incense.

We became very ingenious in thinking up excuses to enable us to stand for a few precious minutes beside the warm stove.

'Please sir, can I put some coal on?' 'Can I poke the fire sir?' 'I think the coals need turning sir.' When allowed to perform one of these longed-for tasks, we'd linger as long as possible and stand toasting ourselves with backsides pressed against the fireguard until ordered back to our seats. How we longed for break time when we could all crowd round the stove. Elsie or Barbara would seek a bucket of water to put on the stove top to boil for our lunch cocoa, providing the rich promise of a warm drink.

My last term at St Peter's was my happiest. Chappie began to teach us book binding. Bill Philipson and I settled down to the job and enjoyed it. We had all the gear; stitching frame, needles, glue pot, strawboard, bookbinder's cloth, a vice a wooden mallet and wood chisels for trimming edges. When we finished our first volume of *Harmsworth's Encyclopaedia* in green cloth with black corners we were very proud. Frequently I found the entries engrossing and spent more time reading than working.

Autumn term came to an end. The leavers shook hands with Chappie, said goodbye, then set off for home. Going home along the Swinhope Lonnen on this dark and gloomy day before Christmas, the day I'd looked forward to for so long, I did not experience the happiness I'd expected.

Red in Tooth and Claw

Mother was extremely fond of animals but their mishaps caused her great distress. Perhaps the circumstances of her childhood, growing up without love, may have produced the feeling she had for animals, but whatever the reason, the anguish she experienced because of this sensitivity to their sufferings was sometimes a blight on her life.

When we first arrived in Swinhope, Mary Liddle gave Mother a male ginger kitten which she named Sandy. It had an extra toe on each foot and was remarkably intelligent. When Mother went for a walk it trotted alongside her like a dog. Sandy learned how to open the kitchen door by leaping up and striking the thumb-plate of the sneck with a downward blow of his paw. Visitors who saw this trick were astonished and would remark, 'My, that's a clever cat.' He was a great hunter, chiefly of rabbits, yet he never attempted to hurt the young chicks that frequently invaded the kitchen to peck up crumbs.

One evening Sandy dragged himself home after being crushed by a large stone or some other heavy object and died the next day. By some strange irony, Mother's pets often ended their lives in ways that caused Mother much distress.

'Here's a clocker for tha.' Annie Sarah Featherstone, a neighbour, stood at our cottage door holding by the legs a plump Rhode Island Red hen which kept on attempting to put its head the right way up. 'She's always clocking. I've dipped her in the well a few times, but it makes no difference. She'll do to set you off with a few hens.'

This kind gift of a broody hen began what eventually became a weird assortment of poultry. Mother was delighted with the hen and called her Annie. We never parted with Annie and she

mothered countless broods. Fortunately we already had a snug
stone hen house with an iron roof, so Annie was put on a clutch of
eggs the very next day.

Mother liked to experiment by putting eggs from various
sources under Annie and in time we had a remarkable variety of
fowls: Rhode Island Reds, Wyandottes with combs like little
crowns, Speckled Leghorns, Minorcas, Buff Orpingtons and
Plymouth Rocks.

When Wharton's bus company began a service to Hexham,
Mother paid occasional visits to the market and would buy a few
eggs just to find out what the result would be. Some of the
hatchings from these random purchases produced birds with
bright and exotic plumage of breeds unknown to anyone in
Swinhope, some with feathery legs and others with wide downy
upper legs giving the impression they were wearing plus fours.

Once Mother tried a few duck eggs from Hexham but only

one bird hatched out. Influenced by a history lesson at school, Norman called the duckling Sir Francis. When it first took to the water in the little stream behind the cottage, Annie the hen was very perturbed and clucked out loud warnings!

We kept a cockerel, hatched from an egg bought in Hexham, which seemed to be a descendant of the fighting cocks of former times. He grew very big with a bright erect comb like the hackle on the cap of a Northumberland Fusilier, red floppy wattles matching his comb and strong sharp spurs on his long yellow legs. He was very proud of his beautiful wing feathers and arched tail. He would pause in his strutting to preen his outstretched wing feathers like a gentleman adjusting his shirt cuffs or flicking a speck of fluff from his sleeve. We named him Charlie.

Charlie was very fond of bread dough. On baking days he would hang around the front door, keeping a sharp look out with his bright eyes for the kitchen door being left open. Then he would dart into the kitchen and peck at the dough left in tins on the fender to rise. Mother used to chase him out, swiping at him with a wet dishcloth. He would dodge round the table squawking with indignation, his beak covered in sticky dough. Sometimes she threw a cushion at him or pushed him outside with the long handled brush shouting, 'Get out, you horrible beast!' As she pushed, he walked backwards pecking furiously at the brush head. Once outside he would crow defiantly before resuming his arrogant walk, pausing now and again to raise a leg and clench his foot as if threatening revenge.

On fine warm days, the hens scratched out hollows under the gooseberry bushes for dust baths. They would lie in these baths flicking dust over themselves with their wings, all the while giving out a happy crooning sound; a kind of henny opera chorus, prima donnas singing as they bathed. Charlie swaggered about viewing his harem and, now and then, selecting one for lovemaking. The favoured hen would let out outraged clucks at being disturbed in her tub and attempt to escape, but Charlie would hold her with his beak and she would have to submit. After this, he would flap his wings, stretch his neck and crow. Sometimes for a change he would make love to Sir Francis after which Sir Francis would run to the little stream and plunge in as if to wash away the disgrace. Later Sir Francis lost his knighthood when we found out he had laid eggs in the stream. J.V. Hill was interested in our weird collection of hens and when he called with his order book, always had a good laugh at the 'drake' which laid eggs. 'How's the drake laying?' he would ask and let out some laughing gas.

I retain a vivid memory of Mother sitting on fine days on the flat stone wall, mixing hen crowdy in a bucket with a stick. The crowdy consisted of bran, boxings, Sussex ground oats and Indian meal mixed in particular proportions, potato skins boiled in a bucket on the fire, and a tiny pinch of Karswood Poultry Spice.

As she mixed the crowdy and made occasional swipes with the stick to ward off the hungry hens, she would sing snippets from the few songs she knew. Items from pre-war musicals such as *The Arcadians, Merry England* and *The Bohemian Girl*. 'It's eighty in the shade they say – tra-la-la-la,' and 'When other lips and other hearts – tra-la-la-la.' I never hear these tunes without a pang of regret for times past.

When Charlton, the aggler as Mother called him, came to Swinhope, she sold him eggs and sometimes a cock chicken or an old hen for a pound of butter. I remember going to the hen house on dark evenings with a torch to find the bird selected, and all the fluttering and squawking of protest as I seized the victim. Charlie would make an awful row and I was always wary in case he pecked my face, but fortunately the light of the torch and the unexpectedness of the abduction seemed to make him incapable of action and I would carry the poor bird down to where Charlton stayed with his cart at the bottom of the bank. As the cart moved away, driven by his son, Charlton began plucking chickens bought on his round, leaving behind a wake of wind-blown feathers.

Once Mother decided to keep a nanny-goat, which Joe Noble allowed her to graze in the pasture adjoining our cottage. Its placid-looking eyes belied its real nature, for it was full of malice and mischief. It frequently either chewed through the tethering rope or hauled the stake out of the ground and went on the rampage. It would leap over dykes into neighbouring meadows, nearly strangling itself when the rope became entangled between big stone copes. It ravaged gardens, and once it chewed the lower parts of shirts, petticoats and sheets hanging out to dry. I would often have to chase and recapture it. It liked to climb on the roof, finding it quite easy to jump the couple of feet to the lower edge of the roof at the back of the house, and stand on the ridge with its nose near the chimney, appearing to enjoy inhaling the smoke.

With Charlie and the goat it was hate at first sight. The goat's ambition was to flatten the bird against the dyke. Whenever she saw him pecking about between herself and the dyke, she would drop her head and charge at full speed, but Charlie would give a nimble side slip with his wings outstretched and peck at her head with quick jerky movements as if he were knocking in nails, as she passed. The frustrated goat would wheel about and charge again, but Charlie would dodge like a matador playing a bull and knock a few more nails in as she rushed by.

Mother gave a shriek as the deck chair collapsed. The cup of tea flew out of her hand and she lay on her back on top of the chair. The goat had seen the deck chair as a tempting target and charged the bulging canvas. This was one trick too many, so Mother sold the goat for a few shillings and was glad to be rid of it, regretting only the loss of the rich milk.

Charlie's combative tendencies became worse. He would

climb on to the ridge of the roof and crow defiance to the whole world. Sometimes a cock at Hope Head, about half a mile away, would answer him and the crowing contest would go on for some time. He began to attack anyone who came to the house. The postman was a particular enemy and he had to defend himself with his stick as Charlie flew at his legs.

'Th'll have to wring his neck, Ada,' he would say. 'He's a bad un.' Mother postponed the awful decision for a long time, but one day he flew at the face of a traveller who had called for the store order and she faced the fact that something had to be done. Our neighbour Robson Hull killed him for us. We had not the heart to prepare Charlie for dinner, so I buried him under a bush in the garden. He looked smaller than in life, his wattles and comb had turned blue but his plumage was just as splendid.

Mother had reverence for all life, yet she could prepare rabbits or cock chickens without squeamishness; she recognised the necessity and got on with the job that had to be done. When the choice was a cock chicken or nothing for a meal, she would ask Robson Hull to kill one for us; she was never able to do the job herself.

Annie, the always-broody hen, would come into the kitchen with her chicks when they were small and peck for crumbs in the clippy mats. Mother was loath to chase them out. The sight of Annie with her family gave her great pleasure.

When some chicks failed to get out of the shell at hatching time, Mother would carefully pick away the shell and membrane of the eggs to get them out. She laid them on a bed of cotton wool in a cardboard box and kept them alive by dipping their beaks in milk. This nearly always worked and the chicks were soon able to run about with the rest of the hatching. Once a chick broke a leg and she mended it using matchsticks as splints and binding it with thread. The chick recovered, but always had a stiff leg, and when

Mother banged the crowdy bucket with a stick at feeding time, all the hens would come running with the stiff-legged one bringing up the rear like the lame boy in the story of *The Pied Piper of Hamelin*.

A woman bearing the strange name of Bithynia once gave Mother a dog. The name Bithynia must, I think, have been obtained by the old-time method of pricking with a pin and eyes closed at the page of a randomly opened Bible. She and her brother Naaman farmed at White Riggs, on the opposite side of Swinhope from where we lived. When Naaman died, she gave my brother, then aged about six, a very small packet of black minty sweets to sit by the corpse while she went away on some errand. After the funeral she gave Mother the black and white collie called Bob. I had often seen the dog chained to a kennel as I passed White Riggs farm, and once I had seen it sitting on the window sill with the lace curtain draped around its head, looking like an old lady wearing a shawl.

Bob had rheumatic legs which eventually became so bad that he could hardly walk.

Jack Reed heard about Mother's predicament and called at our cottage to look at the poor dog. 'Aye it'll have to be shot, Ada, but don't worry lass. I'll do it for you and bury him on the fell.' Jack called later and took the animal away. Mother sat in a chair by the fire, wiping the tears from her eyes.

Harvest Home

During the harvest time when I was thirteen I spent much of the summer at Joe Parker Reed's farm and he began to entrust me with more important jobs. After Joe Parker had marked out a set at the top end of the meadow by driving round a couple of times, he risked letting me take over. I stood beside the machine listening to Joe's instructions and tingling to begin. I had been working for Joe for as few weeks now and I was delighted to be allowed to do horse work. Driving the horse gave me great pleasure and made me feel important.

'Now, th' thinks th' can manage?' he asked. I stepped onto the red-painted axle casing with McCormack stamped on it and fitted myself into the shaped iron seat. It was like sitting in a very large soup spoon. Joe handed me the rope reins. I clicked my tongue, flicked the reins gently over the horse's powerful haunches, and the

machine moved off with a loud whirring noise from its cutting blades. The horse knew very well what to do and required only a slight pull on a rein to direct him. I was wearing my new tweed knickerbockers with horizontal pockets that Mother had bought for me from J.V. Hill in anticipation of my earning a little money, and Alice had given me a blue and white spotted handkerchief to shield my neck from the sun. I felt very grown up and I wished Mother could see me.

Joe watched me at work for a while and then, giving me a wave of his arm to show approval, set off to join Alice, his wife, and Vera, his daughter, who were turning the swathes of the previous day's mowing with hand rakes to open up the undersides to the hot sun.

It was a very hot July morning with a blue sky and a few cauliflower clouds. As I drove along the top edge of the set towards the farmhouse I could see the smoke from the kitchen drifting skywards with hardly a kink in it, and the blue striped mattress Alice had draped over the windowsill of the bedroom to get a good airing. The red and white cows and calves grazing in the pastures on the other side of the dyke watched the mowing machine with intense curiosity. They stood complacently chewing, their silky lips moving steadily from side to side until the machine drew near them and then they'd take fright and scamper, snorting and stopping to fling out their hind legs as if in contempt or defiance.

I was so engrossed in my job that I did not notice the passage of time and I was surprised when I saw Joe coming up the meadow waving his arm and shouting, 'Bait time!'

We unyoked the horse, whose flanks were flecked with white foamy sweat where the harness had rubbed. He kept on shaking his head to shift the flies from his eyes and kicking at his belly to shift the clags.

'We'll leave the collar on, Tom, then we'll not have to catch him again.' He folded the reins and looped them over the harness and the horse immediately began to munch the shorn grass.

After finishing the swathe turning, Alice and Vera had sought our lunch from the farmhouse. Alice removed the white cloth from the large wicker basket, spread it on the ground, and at once the air was fragrant with the smell of pastry and sun-warmed bread and butter and scones. Vera poured the tea for us from blue enamel cans. The hot tea brought out the sweat and I wiped my brow with my shirtsleeves. Alice cut into the creamy brown bacon and egg pie decorated with leaves and acorns, and passed round pieces on the knife blade.

In spite of the heat Alice and Vera were dressed, as usual, in white pinafores, long black skirts, black cotton stockings and clogs with steel buckles. Alice wore a floppy white dust cap but Vera was bareheaded with her long black hair tied behind her head with a blue ribbon. They both knelt on the ground to eat, with skirts tucked under their knees. Joe sat leaning his back against a pike of hay with his knees drawn up and his floppy straw hat pulled down over his eyes. He ate very little and was soon cutting twist tobacco from an old Oxo tin, worn shiny with use, that he kept in the pocket of his multi-patched waistcoat. He teased the thin slices of twist between his cupped hands and filled his clay pipe. The pipe lighted, he contentedly blew out clouds of blue grey smoke and refreshed his mouth from time to time with sips of tea. The horse had made its way down the meadow. As it grazed, its collar slipped down its neck and it would jerk the collar back onto its shoulders with a rattling of the harness.

'Come on now lad, eat th' fill,' Alice said and passed me the remaining piece of gooseberry tart on the knife blade.

'Crop for any corn,' teased Vera with a smile that softened the edge of her mockery.

Later in the afternoon when I'd finished mowing the set, we began sweeping the dried hay to make pikes. We swept uphill, as the pikes would be nearer the barn for leading in. I enjoyed this job, urging the horse uphill with my heels and shouts and clinging to its mane. Joe flung up the handles of the sweep to make a great heap of hay for piking. When all the raked rows were swept, the horse was left to graze and Joe showed me how to make pikes. Vera climbed on top of the pike to trample it firm as we forked on the hay and when only a couple of forkfuls were needed to finish it off she leant on my shoulders to jump down. I felt for a moment a brief intimacy with her. Joe showed me how to finish off a pike by raking it smooth and giving it a few taps with the back of the rake.

'I like to see them standing tidy-like,' he said, 'then the rain will run off.' He took a handful of hay and smelt it. 'This is the natural herb. Better than seed hay where the ground has been ploughed and seeded. This smells sweeter and the kine like it more.'

'Th's snapped it, th' great gowk' Vera cried. I was twirling the rake as she had shown me while she fed in the hay with her hands as a spinner feeds wool to make a thread, but I hadn't the knack and my jerky movement of the rake had snapped the rope. She stood close beside me and demonstrated how to twirl the rake. Putting my hands the proper distance apart on the handle, she held the rake with me.

'Like this seest th', nice and easy like.' She giggled a bit and knelt down to feed the hay as I tried again. 'Th's a great gowk,' she said again, but the tone of her voice was intimate and friendly. I began to get the feel of the job and as I walked slowly backwards with the lengthening rope, I cast covert and admiring glances at Vera kneeling in front of me. I felt a longing for a closer friendship, but did not know what to say. The rope finished, we

tied a large stone on each end and put it over the pike to hold and
help it settle.

We worked at pike-making all that hot afternoon and by the
time the sun was dipping down behind Killhope Moor the last pike
was made.

Joe was very pleased. 'We've won some grand hay now. A few
mair a' these fine days and we'll have it all in.'

The womenfolk went into the house to prepare supper, and,
after stabling the horse and giving it a couple of handfuls of oats, I
joined Joe at the water trough to wash. Joe had stripped to the
waist and was leaning over the trough with his arms immersed to
his shoulders. His sunburnt arms and neck contrasted sharply with
his white back.

'Have a dook,' he invited. 'This is a fine way to cool off.' I
stripped off my shirt and plunged in my arms shoulder-high,
rejoicing in the feel of the soft cool spring water. I thrust my face
under and held it in the water as long as I could. My neck and
forearms burned when I dried them.

The farmhouse kitchen was very comfortable, especially in the
dusk of a summer's day when there was a pool of light from the
oil lamp that hung on a ceiling beam over the bare wood table.
The flames from a small summer fire were reflected in the glass
door of the mahogany press against the wall opposite. The shining
black-leaded fireplace with its steel fender and polished fire irons
added to the feeling of comfort. A grandfather clock stood in the
corner and in the dusky lamplight looked like a man standing with
his feet together and his arms behind his back. There was an oval
brass plate for his mouth that stated 'Reed, Hexham 1849'. It had
a tick like a low moan.

'He's nigh on three hours fast,' explained Joe when he saw me
gazing at the clock. 'He gains about three minutes a day, but he
doesn't like being touched so we let him bide.' I tried to work out

how long it would take before the clock was right again but the sum was beyond me.

I was sitting on the horsehair sofa by the window, still watching Alice and Vera preparing supper. Alice was cutting bread by holding the loaf against her plump bosom and drawing the knife towards her while Vera brought in crockery and food from the back kitchen. I could smell the pink and white potted geranium on the windowsill behind me, which Alice had told me was called Maiden's Blush. I was awed by the shotguns that lay beside some horn-handled walking sticks, and a shepherd's crook, on the lathes screwed across the brown beams, and by two large black and white china cats on the mantelpiece smirking down at the supper table.

'Come on lad, draw up a chair for th'self,' Alice said. I sat down and began buttering bread. 'Now put some on,' she admonished, 'there's God's amount,' and pushed closer the plate piled high with little rolls of butter still beaded with moisture.

'Th' puts butter on like an old spinster,' Joe remarked, and we all laughed. Alice did not sit at the table, but busied herself cutting meat and bread, making more tea, and keeping an eye on us to make sure we had all we needed. I tried to catch Vera's eye to give her a smile but she ignored me completely.

'John's had his supper?' Joe asked. Alice clicked her tongue with irritation and gave a sigh. 'Th' doesn't think I'd forget.'

I often heard reference to John, but apart from his living permanently in a wooden hut in the garden I knew nothing about him and I was too shy to ask questions.

The meal over, Joe withdrew to his Windsor chair by the fire and began to load his pipe. As he teased the tobacco for a fill, he was lost in thought and his brown eyes seemed to reflect some deep inner sadness. Vera sat with her elbows on the table, her chin resting in her cupped hands, while Alice sipped from her mug of tea at the fireside. The only sound was the moaning tick of the old clock. It was dark outside now. I knew it was time to depart, but the feeling of comfort and well being induced by the good meal, and the rest after labour and the family feeling held me and I was loath to move.

'Time for the wooden hill' Joe said and lit a candle in the red enamel candlestick.

Vera stood up and stretched herself and caught hold of the clothes airer just above her head. I looked at her with admiration.

'Vera!' Alice reproved her.

'Th'd best see Tom out,' Joe said. 'We'll lead in tomorrow if the weather holds'.

At the door Vera tugged at the lock of hair on my forehead, said 'Goodnight peewee,' and closed the door quickly before I could say a word. I stumbled along the path home, rich with my experiences of the day. Ma had left the lamp on the table burning very low. I was as quiet as possible but I knew Ma would be lying awake listening for my return. I put out the lamp and crept into the wall bed where Norman was already fast asleep.

We started leading in the next day, on one of those clear early mornings when every sound, a scythe being sharpened, a dog's bark or the clicking of a mowing machine being turned at the corner of a set, rang out sharply, when all the country smells were strong and rich and the colours of the flowers and the new grass, growing where the hay had been harvested, were vivid and bright.

Joe took me with him for the first few pikes until I got the feel of the job. He showed me how to back the flat hay bogie with its broad iron wheels right into the base of the pike, run out the chain from its roller at the front of the bogie and fasten it around the pike. I enjoyed every part of this task, even the hard part of winding on the pike with the keeper on the cog wheel clanging out resonantly on every cog as the pike slid onto the bogie until its weight brought down the flat top with a bang. After leading in a few pikes, Joe allowed me to seek them on my own while he forked the hay into the barn. I felt a delightful sense of adventure and achievement as I stood on the bogie leaning my back against the pike, the reins in my hand and clicking my tongue to encourage the horse.

In the afternoon Joe's nephew Maurice, who was on the six-to-two shift at Sipton lead mine, came to help. Maurice was a young man in his late twenties, not very tall but broad shouldered and immensely strong. He had fair, almost ginger hair and his face, neck and forearms were brick red. He had gained fame as a wrestler.

'Now Tom, woulds't th' fork back and Vera can tread the mow?' Joe asked. Maurice cupped his hand for my foot and threw me up into the space beside the open barn door overhead.

'Th'll never make a wrestler lad,' Maurice said. 'You might make a runner though, or a jockey.'

They all laughed, and the laughter stung me a little.

'Good stuff in small bundles,' Joe remarked and smiled encouragingly.

Maurice seized a hayfork, spat on his hands and threw it from one hand to the other. The polished tines flashed in the sunlight. Then he thrust the fork vigorously into the top of the pike as though he hated it. The fork made a crunching sound and he lifted a great forkful of hay with a smooth and easy movement to where I was waiting in the barn doorway above. I worked furiously to keep the doorway clear, forking up the hay onto the mow above me where Vera was lolloping about sinking in the soft hay up to her thighs as she speared it evenly and trampled it down. Fortunately the distance the bogie had to travel to seek a pike was increasing each time and this gave me a chance to catch up and have a breather.

My feelings towards Maurice were finely balanced. I admired his strength and skills. But I was wary of him because of his taunting remarks, particularly when Vera was present. Once when it had rained heavily through the night and haymaking had ceased for the time being, I went with him to the lower part of the meadow near the burn where the ground was too steep for machine mowing to watch him mow with a scythe. He put two bottles of water in the ditch to keep cool. 'Wish it had been beer,' he said regretfully. He folded his jacket and put it on the ground then began sharpening his scythe, holding the upright in the palm of his hand and stroking the blade with rapid and rhythmic movements of the whetstone. He began to mow, swinging his scythe in a wide swishing arc that left a neatly feathered swathe of lush grass mingled with meadowsweet, marsh marigold and a few spotted orchids. Once his scythe top caught an unlucky frog and impaled it. He paused for a moment and watched it making helpless swimming movements and then flicked it onto the ground and killed it.

'Now let the scythe do the work, Tom.' Maurice was letting me have a go while he had a drink and a smoke. The sun was now

climbing high and the air was sweet with the smells of the swathes and the shorn ground. He leaned back, propping himself on his elbows, and watched my clumsy attempts with an amused and superior grin. He had taken off his shirt and his braces dangled like a pair of handles.

'Lean forward an' let it swing. Take it nice and easy like.' When he took the scythe again, he suddenly leant towards me and said in a confidential way, 'She's a lovely lass is our Vera. I see th' has th' eye on her.' He grinned at my embarrassment. I wriggled a bit inwardly and was startled that he knew my secret longings.

One episode concerning Maurice has etched itself onto my memory. The horse had gone lame and he asked me to hold the bridle while he examined the hoof. He moved towards the leg, patting it gently and warily and speaking softly, but as he got hold of the limb the horse lashed out. Maurice jumped and shouted 'Hang on!' Sparks flashed from the cobble, some speckled leghorns picking among the hayseeds fled with outraged squawks and a ginger cat skedaddled across the yard and leapt the dyke like a steeplechaser. I hung on grimly while Maurice sought a stick with a leather thong at the end. He placed the thong about the horse's muzzle and twisted it tight. 'Now hold it Tom,' he said, and tried to approach again but the horse still kicked and reared high, hoisting me off the ground. For a moment I dangled from the bridle, looking at its wicked yellow teeth and its mouth twisted into a sneer by the thong. Maurice put a few more turns on the stick and warned me to hang on tight. This time the horse did not rear or kick but its flanks and haunches quivered like jelly. Maurice coolly lifted the leg and put the hoof between his knees like a farrier. 'No'but a sliver of stone,' he said, and began to prise it out with his knife.

Everyone laughed now that it was all over. 'By God,' said Joe, 'you very nigh went over the house top. He has a mean streak that horse. He once picked the sleeve right out of my jacket!'

The late afternoon sun was now streaming through the narrow ventilation slits high in the barn wall, beaming shafts of dusty light across the barn. The mow had nearly reached the roughly adzed joists that held up the roof timbers. It was stuffy and hot near the roof and we breathed the smell of old mouldy hay that clung to the roof and its timbers. The confined space and semi-darkness gave me a feeling of intimacy with Vera. I had a sensation of being shut away from the world, and longed to establish a closer relationship, but I did not know how to begin. I heard the crunching noise of the bogie's iron wheels on the cobbles below and Maurice's shouts to the horse. The last pike of the harvest had arrived.

I was astonished and delighted when Vera suddenly decided to ride with me up the high pasture where I took the horse when the day's work was over. She had never done this before. Using a through stone in the dyke for mounting, she sat astride behind me and encircled my waist with her arms. Her nearness made me tingle. As the track sloped steeply uphill I clung to the horse's mane. Vera dug her heels into the horse's sides and he broke into a tired trot. Our elongated shadows joggled about the track ahead and his hooves clumped on the sun-baked mud. I was aware of the smell of hay clinging to Vera's hair as she moved her head closer to mine. When we arrived at the pasture gate Vera slid down nimbly and opened it. I released the horse and he galloped a few yards, rolled on the ground moving his legs and then gave a shrill whinny.

Vera was already running down the track with that strange knock-kneed run girls have, as if kicking out the ground behind her. I set of after her but I couldn't make up the start she had and she got back before me.

As I entered the kitchen Alice was leaning towards the oven door and sliding a great pie with two pastry funnels from the oven shelf. I sat beside Maurice, who was sitting on the sofa with his legs outstretched and a glass of beer in his hand. There were some full bottles with pictures of machine guns on their labels on the table and some empties on the floor. Maurice stared at the huge pie with the wisps of fragrant steam coming from its funnels and said 'Gar bon, a battleship.' We all laughed and Alice gave Maurice a playful clout over the head with her oven cloth. Maurice stood up and said in a mock posh voice, 'I name this ship HMS *Alice*. God bless all who sail in her.'

'Sit down th' great gowk,' Alice said and began cutting and serving the deck of the battleship pie. Maurice poured me a glass of beer which tasted horrible to me but I pretended to like it. Suddenly the thought came to me that now the harvest was over I'd not be needed.

'Th' looks pretty glum lad,' Maurice said. 'Has Vera been bullying you?'

Alice cut me some more pie and must have sensed my thoughts for she invited me to come along and have a bit of crack with John.

After supper I set off home, sad at heart with the thought of starting school again the following week, but the last picture in my mind as I fell asleep that night was of Vera astride the horse with me, her arms encircling my waist and her face close to mine as we rode up the track to the high pasture.

My Pal John

After harvest time I had an opportunity to meet Joe Parker Reed's son, John.

'Now Tom, woulds't th' like to meet John and have a bit crack?' Alice asked. I was very curious about John. I'd overheard fragments of talk and had seen Alice carrying his meals, but I'd been told nothing directly and was too diffident to ask the questions that were itching in my mind. Ma had told me that he must be very ill and had to live in the hut to help him get better.

'Here's Tom to see th',' Alice said as she opened the door, and indicating the chair by the bedside, began adjusting the pillows and smoothing the blue and white quilt, making mock complaint by clicking her tongue as she did so.

Alice left us and John stretched out a pallid hand to grasp mine lightly and asked 'How ist th'?' John was a young man in his early twenties, very thin and pale, but his hair was black and glossy and his large brown eyes very lively.

We were both quiet for a while; he like myself I think, dredging in his mind for something to say. I looked about me and felt a tingle of excitement when I saw a row of books and some magazines on a white painted shelf beside his bed, and on a little table a wireless set with its earphones hanging over the rail of his bed. A small oil lamp with a coloured glass bowl and a fluted brass stem stood on the table beside a pair of binoculars. The floor was bare apart from a brightly coloured clippy mat near the bed. In spite of the bareness the books and other articles gave the hut a strangely rich atmosphere.

It was now autumn and ragged white clouds were racing across the skyline on the opposite side of the dale. I found that if I gazed intently at the clouds I felt a sensation of movement as if the hut were being whisked away by an unknown force, towards an unknown destination, a feeling enhanced by the occasional gusts of wind rattling the windows.

John put on the headphones and made some adjustments to the wireless set then handing them to me asked if I would like to listen. I sat with the earphones on, enthralled with the dance music. This was the very first time I had heard the wireless.

The music ended and I reluctantly handed back the earphones. Then John said 'Woulds't th' like an Edgar Wallace?' I took the lurid yellow paperback with its picture of the body of a murdered man lying on the floor beside the murder weapon, a candlestick, and felt a surge of excitement at the anticipation of reading the story. I hurried home with the precious book anxious to tell Ma of my wonderful experience with the wireless.

I became a fairly frequent visitor to John's hut, always hoping that John would ask me to listen in for a while or pass on to me some books he had finished with. Sometimes when I called at the farmhouse to ask permission to visit John, Alice would say, 'John is not very clever today, best not go in.' Then she would offer me a slice of cake or a piece of tart as compensation, and she would discuss bits of gossip with me as I sat eating on the horsehair sofa.

I discovered that John's hut held more for me than books and wireless.

'That's where they found him,' John said, pointing to the open window in the direction of Killhope. 'A shepherd found the coffin sticking out of the peat. When they opened the lid, they saw the body wrapped in a blanket. The peat had preserved him and he still had on his overcoat fastened with lead buttons.'

I listened intently as John related the story in his gentle voice. The story gripped my imagination and invested Killhope with a quality of mystery. I pictured a scene of men in kilts and plaids

splashing through bogs and stumbling across the ling laden with
the coffin of a dead comrade.

'He was a big man with flaxen hair, and when they lifted him
out of the coffin, the lead bullet that killed him dropped out of the
body. They say he'd been buried a long time, mebbies a couple of
hundred years, and that he must have been a Scots soldier who'd
been fighting in the rebellion. Perhaps he was killed at the battle
near Penrith and his pals carried him over the fell from there.'

'How did they know he was a Jacobite?'

'The rose on the lead buttons, the badge of the Jacobites.'

'What did they do with the body?'

'He's buried over the top of Killhope in Weardale churchyard.'

'Do you think there'll be any more bodies there on Killhope?'

'Aye, mebbies.'

I resolved to keep a sharp lookout for coffins sticking out of
the peat when I was roaming about on Killhope side with my
friend Bill.

The story over, John lapsed into silence and we both stared out
of the window. A blackbird standing under a wet blackcurrant
bush began singing. The rain had stopped and a shaft of mellow
autumn sunshine made a patch of light on John's blue quilt. I was
still thinking about the unknown soldier and wondering why his
friends had buried him on Killhope side.

A relation of John's who lived on Tyneside sent him parcels of
books and magazines from time to time and I also became a
beneficiary. For a long time the books John kindly passed on to me
were my only source of reading. I looked forward to John's parcels
more eagerly than to Christmas. Chiefly a parcel would contain
yellow paperbacks by Edgar Wallace, Sapper, Phillips Oppenheim
and Horning. Some of these authors I'd already become
acquainted with in Gateshead Library, but I discovered new
authors among little chocolate coloured hardbacks sold in

Woolworth's for sixpence. I sat at nights by the single-wick oil lamp completely absorbed in *The Beloved Vagabond* by W.J. Locke, *Captain Salvation* by Lew Wallace, and Conrad's *Typhoon*. I think the thriller writers made the greatest impression and as I had almost no historical knowledge, I thought of Conan Doyle's London and that of Edgar Wallace without any gap between them; Holmes and Watson riding in hansom cabs inhabited the same world as Wallace's Mr Reader who pinned a villain to the ground with the ferrule of an umbrella poised over the miscreant's face, warning him that if he moved a muscle he would lose an eye. I also became acquainted with P.G. Wodehouse but the subtle use of language was over my head and I was more impressed by the fact that Jeeves frequently received tips of five pounds. I was too young to enter the daffy world of Wodehouse. On one occasion, John's lucky dip parcel contained Jack London's *Call of the Wild*. This book made a very deep impression and I ranked it second only to *Robinson Crusoe*.

Sometimes when I visited John he was very quiet and hardly spoke. At other times he was quite lively and would identify various birds he could see through the window and pass me his binoculars for me to observe them. He took great pleasure in watching birds and beasts and a rare visitor such as a heron gave him great joy. I first saw a heron through the window of John's hut, and I was amazed both by its size and what appeared to be its effortless flight. It was following the burn upstream looking for fish, John told me. He taught me the names of the birds and how to recognise their cries.

One gloomy autumn evening when I visited him, John told me the story, famous in the dales, of the great strike of the lead miners in 1849.

'The men worked on contracts, and were paid for the amount of galena they produced. They worked to suit themselves as they had their own farms to work on, but the owners and the agent, Sopwith, wanted them to work regular hours, all the shift workers starting together at stated times. The miners went on strike. A man named Joseph Heslop was their leader. He called the men who gave in and went back to work the regular hours each day, blacklegs, and he spoke fiercely against them at a meeting in Swinhope Chapel. The strike lasted five months and in the end a hundred strikers were sacked.'

I was feeling the glow of interest I experience when hearing of stirring events of the past – when the intervening time melts away and the events seem close and real. I had a clear picture in my mind of Joseph Heslop shouting out his fierce denunciation of the blacklegs as he stood in the little pulpit in Swinhope Chapel where Joe Noble preached about brotherly love.

'What happened then?'

'Most of them migrated to America, and a few to Australia. Sixty folk set out on one day from Liverpool to sail to the United States. They settled on the banks of the Illinois River. I know a girl whose grandfather went out. It took him months to get there she told me.'

When I lived in Gateshead, I had often seen the ships moored on Newcastle quayside and I could easily picture the scene of families climbing aboard up the gangway. Mothers with babies, or small children clinging to their skirts, and men laden with boxes or bags containing a few precious possessions, setting off for life in a new land.

'Why'd the leader call the men who went back to work blacklegs?'

'I'm not sure. Mebbies 'cause when sheep have a disease called blackleg they can't stand up. The blacklegs couldn't stand up for themselves you see.'

'What did the folk do in America when they arrived there?'

'Worked on farms I think, and some went in the coal mines. Perhaps some of them joined the Gold Rush to California. Gold was discovered there the same year they went out.'

I found this a very thrilling idea and imagined who'd mined for lead in the drifts I'd seen in Killhope side panning for gold, as I'd read about in the *Wide World* magazine. I wondered if any had become very rich.

John snuggled a little further into his bed and pulled the bedclothes under his chin and I knew it was time to depart.

'Don't forget Tuesday,' he said, as I was about to go. 'Old Teasdale's coming to give us a tune.'

John's calling Teasdale 'old' was a term of affection rather than an indication of his age, for Bill Teasdale was a very sprightly middle-aged man who enjoyed a great reputation as a fiddle player and teller of droll stories which held listeners on a fine knife edge between belief and disbelief. I hardly knew him except by sight and reputation. I occasionally passed by his little farm and he'd perform a comic mime by picking up a fork or a spade and very solemnly present arms with it. At other times he would salute or put an imaginary stick under his arm and shout 'Stand by your beds!' or 'All present and correct, Sir!' I felt on these occasions that the comedy was perhaps barbed and had always passed by without stopping to chat.

When I arrived at John's hut filled with the excitement of anticipation, Bill was already there and telling John about his misfortune with a pike of hay. He paused for a moment to say 'Hello lad,' and went on with his story.

'Well, I'd very nigh got to the top of the field when the horse faltered a bit and I went to his head to help him on. Just then the damn pike fell off the sledge and rolled right to the dyke at the bottom of the field.' He paused a moment. 'A good job I'd moved from behind the sledge or it would have rolled me down with it in among the nettles.'

Bill Teasdale was a medium sized man with a brown face shading into blue on his high cheekbones. He was wearing cord trousers, brown leggings, and a sleeveless leather jacket over his striped flannel shirt and he had a blue knitted tie around his neck but no collar. I noticed with glee that his fiddle, wrapped inside a piece of cloth that looked like an old curtain, was propped up in the corner.

I was on edge with excitement longing to hear him play, but for a while he kept on talking to John about his farm and how difficult it was to win his hay because of the steepness of the meadows that had to be scythe mown, and how he had to use a sledge to get the hay to the barn.

Then at last he picked up his fiddle, unwrapped it, and nestling it in his lap, began to tune it.

'Hast th' ever seen the blackcock lecking?' he asked. 'Now th' knows the back of my house is right on the fell side. Well, not far

away there is a patch of sheep nibbled grass among the ling. Once, early on in the year, just after I'd had me tea, I chanced to look out of the window at the back and I saw six of them there on the smooth bit of grass. They were all shiny black with bonny red combs and downy legs. When they turned their hint ends towards me their white under feathers looked for all the world like shirt tails flapping about. They stand in a circle, as if for a set of the lancers, and then two of them stamp on the ground and come towards each other with their neck feathers ruffled, bobbing up and down and flapping their wings a bit.' He put down his fiddle and with his hands mimed the jerky movements of the birds.

'It's just like a dance th' knows. Now I'll tell th' what I did. I nipped up to the window and played a bit of a jig and there they were hopping about and enjoying it.'

I found it impossible to tell whether he was serious or joking, but I wanted desperately to believe this enchanting story.

'Now this is the tune I played for them.'

He adjusted the tuning pegs a tiny bit and began to play a very lively jig. I thumped my foot and John tapped his hand on the side of the mattress in time to the tune. The foot thumping made the hut vibrate and the flame leap up in the lamp glass. He moved from tune to tune in quick succession, and after pausing for a moment to put rosin on his bow, remarked 'Aye she's playing well tonight.'

He looked at me and gave a slow wink.

'Fiddles are like women th' knows, not always in the mood.'

Next he played some sad waltz tunes. I felt sad yet happy at the same time and thought how wonderful it was to play a fiddle.

Not long after this musical evening in John's hut his elder brother, Hubert, who worked underground in Sipton lead mine, found me a job in the washing where the lead ore was crushed and the lead separated from the stone.

I did not see John for some time.

One Saturday afternoon when I arrived home from work, Alice was in our cottage talking to Mother. I saw the pain and distress on Mother's face. I knew that look so well. I'd seen it when she heard about cruelty to an animal or a child.

'Tom,' Alice asked, 'Wouldst th' go to Hill's shop up by to get me some black edged envelopes? John has died.' I could find no words to say. I took the proffered money and set off to walk to Hill's shop at Allenheads.

A few days after John's funeral his father, Joe, came to see me and brought a parcel of paperbacks and magazines, John's last bundle which had arrived after his death.

'I thought you would like these, Tom. John would have liked th' to have them and it would have been a shame to burn them.'

This kindness touched me deeply, but I was at a loss how to express myself and was only able to stammer out a simple 'Thank you, Joe.'

The Bike House

One morning Mother was surprised when she opened the front door to find a dead rabbit hanging by its hind legs on the doorknob. The hind legs were tied with a piece of string to a loop over the knob. There was a little pool of blood on the doorstep. Mother made enquiries and found out that it would certainly be Jack Reed who had left the gift of the rabbit. Jack passed our cottage on his way to his bike house and Mother watched out for him to thank him. When she saw him she dashed out and said 'Thank you for the rabbit. We had a lovely pie.'

'What rabbit? Tied on the doorknob you say? I know nowt of it.' He said this without a glimmer of a smile, leaving Mother undecided whether he was pulling her leg or not.

Back in the house Mother would say, 'I'll bet it was Jack though,' as if trying to convince herself.

Jack Reed, of Hope Head farm at the high end of Swinhope, was in his early twenties, a well-made broad-shouldered man with a very kind heart and a sly sense of humour. He several times played the rabbit trick on Mother and always with a stony face denied all knowledge of it. Mother used to click her tongue and say 'Oh dear, he won't let me say 'thank you'.'

Norman and I just laughed and were delighted at the prospect of rabbit pie, a real treat.

We schoolboys in Swinhope, Maurice Liddle, Joseph Noble, Bill Philipson (usually know by his nickname of Little Bogs), and myself, used to listen enthralled to the stories Jack Reed told us in his bike house. We admired him enormously because he owned an AJS motorbike; he was the only person we knew who owned such a thing. How we wished we could emulate him as the bike thundered along Swinhope Lonnen, leaving behind clouds of

limestone dust in the dry weather and on wet days sending out wings of spray as the bike swished through puddles. It was a great thrill to be given a ride on his pillion seat, cleaving through the air at great speed, leaving in our wake a great roar of noise that reverberated right through the dale to the foot of Killhope and sent cattle and hens skedaddling across the roadside pastures. I recall clinging on with fear and delight as Jack took the sharp bends at speed, his handlebars brushing the long grass by the roadside, and my gasp of relief as the bike became upright again.

Jack kept his AJS in the bike house, a little stone building with a green-lichened flagstone roof by the burnside at Swinhope Mill. There in the old days, I was told, the lead miners used to grind the corn they bought at Hexham. Between the bike house and the barn there was a whole forest of nettles and some frothy meadowsweet. My pals and I would congregate in this little dank house, listening to the tales that Jack told us. We sat on pieces of wood, our backs against the wall, breathing in the strange smell compounded of engine oil, petrol, damp stone, nettles and meadowsweet.

He told us stories of ghosts and hauntings; of the ruins of a cottage, close by the path to Lot Heads where Maurice Liddle lived, called Pasture Nook, which had fallen down when struck by lightning killing the old lady who lived there, and which was, folk said, haunted by her ghost; and of weird events such as the quarryman breaking open a piece of limestone with his hammer and finding a live frog entombed inside – it had lived for three days afterwards.

We boys listened entranced to these stories. Freshets of night air gusted in from time to time through the slightly open door and made the solitary candle burn with a lopsided flame.

The ghost stories tautened my nerves and the wizened hawthorns I passed on the way home took on shapes of menace – black spectres with arms upstretched ready to pounce. One night I stumbled over a sheep sleeping across the path and cried out in fear.

Jack told us the story of 'The Long Pack'. He flicked his cigarette into the gloomy autumn night and began:

'Colonel Ridley, a rich farmer, lived in Lee Hall near Bellingham. Once at the back end of the year he went with his wife to London. He left the bailiff, Richard, and his wife, Alice, in charge. While the colonel was away Richard and Alice lived in the Hall. Late one night, when Richard was out visiting friends in a nearby cottage, Alice heard a knocking on the door. She saw a peddler standing at the doorstep with a long pack on the ground beside him.'

'I'm soaked through to the skin. Can I leave my pack until the morning? I've been lugging it around all day in this filthy weather, I'm fair done in and I'll have to find somewhere to get my head down.'

Alice thought him a rough looking chap but she took pity on

him and felt there could be no harm in having the pack in the Hall overnight. When he'd gone she looked curiously at the pack in the hallway and wondered what was inside. The cat was sniffing round it. She went through to the parlour to sit by the fire till Richard came home.

As Alice sat warming herself, she heard a noise she couldn't place coming from the hallway, a kind of snuffling noise. She lit a candle, crept up to the door, and pushed it open. She heard the noise again and saw the pack move. She ran like a hare to seek Richard. The men ran back to the house with Alice. Richard loaded his big gun he called a Copenhagen. The men moved carefully up to the door with Alice behind them holding the candle and slowly pushed it open. They heard the scuffling noise and the pack moved again.

Richard aimed at the pack and let blaze with the Copenhagen. They saw blood oozing through the cloth wrapping and dribbling across the stone floor. The men opened the pack and found a wrinkled-faced dwarf inside with a knife in his hand. The gunshot had killed him. Round his neck the dwarf was wearing a cord with a silver whistle shaped like a hunting horn attached.

Richard's friend sought aid from the other estate workers and Richard posted them at the upper windows with loaded guns. He then went to the door and gave a loud blast on the dwarf's whistle.

Soon they heard the sound of horsemen approaching the Hall. They'd heard the whistle and thought the door would be open. As soon as the thieves arrived in the yard, the men at the windows let fly with their guns. The gunfire killed three of the men, but the rest rode away and escaped.

A search was made for the men who got away but they were never found. The dead thieves and the dwarf were buried in Bellingham Churchyard where you can see to this day. The dwarf's tombstone is shaped like a peddler's pack.'

Jack told us he had seen the tombstone and this assured us of the truth of the story.

Whenever I hear this tale mentioned I have a vivid picture in my mind of we three boys, sitting hunched up against the bike house wall with our arms hugging our knees, listening to Jack's convincing storyteller's voice by the light of one wavering candle flame and the noise of the burn in flood as a background.

Sometimes Jack talked about motorbikes. I wasn't much interested in the twist grips, saddle tanks and such technical matters, but the names of the bikes seemed a kind of poetry to me: Norton, BSA, Royal Enfield, AJS, Velocette, NUT, Francis-Barnett, Panther, Matchless, Triumph.

I liked it better when Jack told us about local history – about James Radcliffe, Earl of Derwentwater, who had been beheaded for treason, and how the servant who had gone to London to bring back the body had fought with a famous Italian swordsman and killed him.

I enjoyed hearing the story of Heathery Burn Cave near Stanhope where a quarryman had broken into a cave used by Bronze Age people and had found spearheads, axes, horse bits, gold bracelets and a bronze bucket. I was disappointed to learn that the finds had been taken away to London and I wondered if any of these ancient people had lived near Swinhope.

At one time lead miners from Swinhope and nearby places used to work in Nenthead. They would stay there for the working week and return to their homes at the weekends when weather permitted. They had no transport and had to walk both ways. Maurice Liddle's father was killed in an accident in the mine when explosives went off before the men got clear. The roads at this time were completely blocked with snowdrifts, too deep even for a horse to get through. So Jack Liddle's workmates put the coffin and some shovels on a sledge, tied on some ropes and set off on the long road from Nenthead to St Peter's Churchyard at Sparty Lea, a distance of seven miles. The snow blew across the fellside blocking the road with deep drifts where they had to stop to cut out a pathway.

Jack's Liddle's widow, Mary, and some friends, walked from Swinhope to the road to meet the men, but the visibility was so poor because of the driving snow that they missed them, and by the time they had turned back and made their way to St Peter's, the funeral service was over.

I found Jack's account of the epic journey over the highest ground in England in the midst of a dreadful storm very stirring, and it remained always in my mind as an example of the kind of people who lived in the Dales.

A Boy's Paradise

At last Bill Philipson and I had made a raft that would float on Swinhope Head Dam. We had made a couple that floated, but they would not bear our weight. This one kept us afloat, but only just; if we made a hasty movement it capsized and tipped us into the water. We paddled the raft about with pieces of wood as we sat on the edge with our legs dangling in the water.

Swinhope Head Dam had been constructed the previous century to collect water for washing the lead ore obtained from the drifts bored into the flanks of Killhope; but it was a place of isolation and quiet, a place where herons fished and a paradise for boys.

Near the dam grew a large expanse of head-high bracken into which we had made a path and near the centre had trampled the bracken flat to make a kind of green cave. This hideaway was not really necessary as no one ever came near, but we enjoyed the feeling of having a secret place and marked the entrance with white stones. Here we sat on pieces of wood we had dragged in, and ate the sandwiches and drank cold tea from a bottle that Mother supplied, and sometimes smoked cigarettes Bill had been able to cadge from his elder brothers.

Bill and I went on many sorties to ruined houses to find the wood for our raft. We made several journeys carrying the longest pieces we could find and left them by the dam side until we had collected enough to begin work. Not having any tools, we broke pieces of wood by holding the heaviest stone we could lift above our heads and dropping it on a piece we had positioned with one end on a large stone. We also used a stone to hammer in nails. Bill brought some rope and more nails from home, and we used nails

from the old wood when they were not too rusty.

We spent many happy hours paddling our raft to and fro, using it as a diving board and resting on it in the sunshine when we tired of swimming. We moored it by tying it to a stone in a little sandy creek at one end of the dam when we went home. Bill had a plan to borrow a fishing rod from his brother John to catch trout and grill them on a fire, but this plan was postponed because the fine weather ended and when we next visited the dam the raft was gone, washed away during a storm.

One day as we sat talking in our green cave among the bracken, we discussed the haunted house called Pasture Nook where the woman had been killed when the house was struck by lightning. John Liddle told me no one ever went near as it was haunted and that he had seen the ghost, a woman wearing a long black dress and a bonnet, standing where the upstairs window had been. I did not believe in the ghost, but whenever I was going home alone from visiting the Liddles at Lot Heads Farm late at night I always ran past at full speed.

'Do'st th' think there'll be anything left under the stones?' Bill asked. I thought that when the body was taken out people would have taken the money and the stock.

'Aye, mebbies, but perhaps the stones covered everything and they only got the body out.'

We decided that there may still be something there. We also reasoned that the ghost was hardly likely to trouble us in the daytime.

Pasture Nook stood by the side of a footpath leading from the Swinhope road to Lots Head Farm. The wall facing the footpath was almost intact, but the upper part of the back wall had almost crumbled away, the stones which had fallen inward making a pile on top of the flagstones from the roof. Small pieces of rotted floor joists lay among the stones on the floor and crumbling pieces of blue colour-washed plaster lay near the bottom of the wall.

The ruined place rang with noise as we flung stones to the ends of the stone floor. After working for about an hour I felt a tingle of excitement as I saw, between the gaps of the remaining stones, some rotted wood. We bent down together to lift one of the bigger stones. As we did so we heard the sound of footsteps scraping on some loose stones outside. We dropped the stone, clambered up the wall like startled cats and, grabbing the slab of the windowsill, heaved ourselves up to stand where the upper window had been. We saw a man's head and shoulders appear above the ruined end wall. He was wearing a grey jacket and cap. For a few moments he peered about him and then moved off. If he had looked upwards he would have seen us. We watched him until he was out of sight. He never looked back.

We jumped down to continue our search. Though we moved every stone and the pieces of crumbling wood which seemed to have been the counter of the shop, we found only rusty remainders of drawer handles and some packets with the still decipherable word 'Lingfords' on them, containing a powder turned green with mould, and some small folded packets with a picture of a cradle on them. We scraped away the damp rubble very carefully, but there was nothing else. Even the old-fashioned nails with square heads were too rusty to be of any use.

On the way home Bill suddenly stopped. 'Th' knows that bloke had no dog with him, so he couldn't have been on the fell looking for his sheep.' We wondered who the man could be. We were quite sure we had never seen him before. 'Perhaps he was a ghost.' Bill said, and we laughed.

'But we heard his footsteps and he had a walking sick', I said. 'Besides, ghosts just sort of glide about and go through solid walls and the ghost in that house is a woman.'

'If a ghost has clothes on then he could have a walking stick.'

Though I did not believe the ghost theory, I was very puzzled as to his identity. We never did find out who the mysterious visitor was.

We lads in Swinhope wandered as free as birds. The only prohibition was walking across a meadow, otherwise we were free to go where we pleased. We hand-fished for trout in the burn, hunted rabbits, gathered bilberries, searched for mushrooms and harvested gooseberries, blackcurrants and raspberries from the gardens of derelict houses where the nettles and docks grew head high and where startled birds, which had also been feasting, took off with a swish of wings as if launched from a catapult.

In summer we spent many happy timeless hours damming the burn with stones and turves to make dooking pools. In winter we made sledges and skis. We took sledges to Allenheads, where Ted Dodd the blacksmith fitted them with iron runners for sixpence. We curled up the ends of the skis by boiling them in the set pot by the fire and applying pressure to the ends while wedged between two big stones in a dyke. Old pieces of leather nailed to the sides of the skis provided foot straps.

Throwing stones at bottles and tins set up in the quarry face in Thorney Knowe quarry was a favourite pastime. The quarry had not been worked for many years and was used as a rubbish tip where rusty tins, bottles, old oil stoves and bed ends lay among the nettles. Maurice Liddle was the champion at this game. He always threw stones as he walked about and had developed amazing accuracy.

Once, when I had been reading a book by George Borrow, I came across a description of how gypsies gained mastery over a horse by breathing into its nostrils. I told Bill about this and we decided to experiment on a horse to find out if it worked. The horse we selected for enslavement was a glossy black gelding which grazed in a pasture adjoining the fell, well away from the farmhouse of its owner. If all went well we would be able to enjoy some gallops round the pasture without the farmer finding out.

'I suppose that is how gypsies steal horses,' Bill said. 'They won't need to carry a bridle or anything; they'll just breathe into its nostrils and the horse will follow them.'

The horse snuffled a bit at the bran in my cap and began to eat. Bill clapped its glossy neck as it munched. Having finished eating, the horse raised its head. Bill hung on to its mane while I cupped my hand over its nostril and began blowing gently through my hand. Suddenly, the horse reared up thrashing the air with its great hooves and gave out a tremendous whinny. Bill was jerked off his feet and fell on the grass. I stumbled as I leapt backwards to avoid the flailing hooves and fell to the ground. We both scrambled to our feet, streaked to the dyke and jumped over to safety. The horse trotted to the dyke, flung out its hind legs and whinnied again, perhaps as a kind of warning. We never went near that horse again and decided we would not try any more horse whispering.

Bill and my other friends all lived on farms and I frequently joined in farming activities, particularly at harvest time. The farmer's year was punctuated by seasonal occupations, lambing time, sheep-dipping and shearing time, harvest time and pig-slaughtering. Though the farm-bred youngsters often could watch a pig-killing as impassively as they might watch a tree felling, I, a townie with a townie's sensitivity, found the sight of a pig being stunned with a large hammer called a mell and having its throat cut too harrowing. My sensitivity however, did not preclude my enjoyment of the bacon, or links of sausage or black pudding given to me by friendly farmers.

Almost the only other events in the farmers' lives were concerned with Chapel. The passage of time was marked by special services for Easter and Christmas, Harvest Festival and the Sunday School Anniversary. Though only about one third (or less) of the people went to Chapel regularly, almost everyone attended special festivals.

We lads enjoyed the festivals in the little chapel. We savoured the excitement and sense of occasion and indulged in a bit of flirting with the girls, who looked very attractive in their best dresses and new hair ribbons. Sometimes a girl was apprehensive about the close proximity of certain characters in the pew behind her and would turn round. Then we would put our chins on the pew back and grin like gargoyles.

At every Harvest Festival Joe and Mary Noble sang their duet standing in the little pulpit: 'Bringing in the sheaves, sowing seeds of kindness, bringing in the sheaves.' Joe accompanied with his concertina which he swung round in large circles for greater effect. This was followed by the congregation singing 'All things bright and beautiful', accompanied by the asthmatic harmonium played by a lady wearing a black straw hat adorned with cherries that flopped about as she swayed from side to side to pump more air into the harmonium. After the service we rushed into the little room adjoining the chapel to feast on the good things brought by the womenfolk: scones with farm-made butter in decorative pats, home-made jam, teacakes, tarts and the fruitcake called spice loaf.

At the Chapel Anniversary Service, boys and girls performed on squeaky fiddles, sang and recited poems about David the shepherd boy, Samson, and other dramatic Bible characters. A visiting preacher would preach a long sermon which made us squirm and wriggle on the pitch pine pews and long to be outside.

One year during the sermon a couple of boys released some bees, previously captured in a jam jar, through the open window at the back of the chapel. The preacher, with sweeping gestures and grave tones, struggled on bravely to tell the people about Mordecai and Hamen, but he found it difficult with half his congregation playing impromptu badminton with hymn books and enraged bees, while the other half jerked their heads from side to side as fascinated spectators.

On dark, cold Sunday evenings, the little iron stove standing below the pulpit glowed red while the brass oil lamp, hanging from the ceiling by a chain, cast a circle of light above – perfect symbols of Heaven and Hell during hellfire sermons. Joe Noble always said a prayer before the last hymn for the young and rising generation. When Joe Noble or a visiting preacher read from the Bible or said prayers, their words sounded perfectly natural as their everyday speech was very close to the language of the Bible.

One year the Chapel people arranged an outing to Whitley Bay. We were all very excited at the prospect of going on such a long journey and a visit to the seaside. We met at the Chapel and walked to the bottom of Sparty Lea bank, which was the nearest place Joe Dixon from Allendale could drive the charabanc. It was a lovely June morning with a few cauliflower clouds in the sky. We could see the smoke rising straight up from newly-lit fires in the farmhouse kitchens. Joe folded back the canvas hood and we climbed aboard. Mothers, with baskets of provisions over their arms, cuffed boys fighting for coveted seats near the driver. Joe gave the starting handle a few quick turns and the engine throbbed. We were off, leaving behind us little clouds of limestone dust. We cheered and waved at a man breaking stones by the roadside, a woman milking a goat tethered on the grass verge and a farmer repairing a dyke. Mothers passed round packets of black bullets, liquorice allsorts and Dainty Dinah toffees hoarded for the occasion.

Eva Reed's mother had entrusted her with a dozen eggs and a plucked chicken to deliver to some friends in South Shields. The mothers held a conference when we arrived in Whitley Bay and decided it would be better to stay together as a party so that no one would get lost. We all boarded the open topped tramcar that would take us to North Shields Pier where the ferryboat crossed the river to South Shields.

My first time afloat. The boat shook as the screw bit the river, churning up yellow water and dirty smells. The steam whistle blasted out a warning and we moved away from the quay. We lads dashed about, anxious to see everything, peeped down the skylight to watch the movement of the pistons and leaned over the rails to view the tugs and small craft in the river. A bell rang, the engine stopped and the ferryboat glided the last few yards, bumped against the rope fenders and everyone rushed for the gangway.

The mothers shepherded us into a group and we set off to find the house of Eva's friends. We trudged up and down streets that all looked alike. People we asked did not know or were very vague. Our precious time was running away. At last we found the place and Eva delivered the chicken and eggs.

Our spirits revived a little as we made the return ferry journey and boarded the tram for Whitley Bay. There we discovered to our dismay that it was almost time to meet Joe Dixon. We had not even dipped our feet in the sea, had a ride on a donkey or got sand in our shoes. All we had seen of the sands was the glimpses from the top of the tram.

On the way home my cap blew off. Joe stopped the charabanc and I dashed back along the road. I saw a man standing by the side of the road leaning on his stick. I said to him breathlessly, 'Have you seen it?'

'Not yet laddie, but I live in hope,' was his strange reply. I could not find my cap and had to return without it. I told Mother and Annie Sarah what the man by the roadside had said and they both broke into unquenchable laughter – I could not understand what they were laughing about. The joke was relayed back from seat to seat until everyone was laughing. We young ones, not wanting to miss anything, joined in.

Everyone started singing. We sang all the way home that lovely June evening and felt that we had had a great adventure.

The Burnfoot Show took place once a year. It was sited on a flat field near the burnside and people arrived at the show on foot, horseback and with pony and trap. The beer tent, where farmers met friends they rarely saw, was very popular. To us youngsters hanging around outside, peeping in or chasing each other round it and tripping over the guy ropes, it seemed a mildly sinful attraction. Men in hairy grey suits and brown leggings and with ram's horn handled sticks over their arms slapped each other on the back, shook hands heartily and shouted loud greetings of 'How ist th'?', 'Hows th' fettle?', 'Ist th' keeping gaily?'

A strong smell of beer and twist pipe tobacco floated out of the tent doorway to mingle with the smell of trampled grass. No woman ever visited the beer tent – that would have been improper and as Dalespeople said, 'Not menseful'.

We young ones would file through the tents where the home and garden produce was displayed and looked hungrily at the tempting show of bread and cakes, scones and teacakes. The fruit tarts had decorated pastry sprinkled with sugar, each with a neat little edge cut out for the judge's tasting. Red, blue or yellow cards spiked the winning entries. There were small baskets of red currants and black, raspberries and amazing gooseberries as big as plums; green, red and yellow varieties, some hairy, some smooth.

The Cumberland-style wrestling matches provided the highlight of the show. The contestants were dressed in vividly striped tights, each in his own particular colours. The opponents would face each other with chin on the adversary's right shoulder. They would fling their arms round each other's back to obtain good hand lock and slowly stamp on the ground for a foothold. They looked like a weird four-legged animal dancing to the tune of the Dead March. When the umpire gave the signal the striving began, each attempting to make his opponent touch the ground with some part of his body other than his feet. They would try back heel throws, or a cross buttock throw, or sometimes give a sudden twist and lift the opponent off the ground before throwing him. Occasionally they both came crashing to the ground together, the one who touched the ground first being the loser.

The wrestling over, there would be races for youngsters, music from the brass band and folk gathered in the tea tent to gossip, meet old friends and feast on the vast variety of home-made foodstuffs and tea prepared in a nearby farmhouse and carried to the tea tent. The tent was full of laughter and the hum of many conversations all muddled together, the smell of food and the special smell of tea made in an urn.

At Christmas time we went guising. We dressed ourselves in whatever we could get hold of to make a comic outfit. For a few days beforehand we made and painted masks from cardboard or pieces of cloth, beards from sheep's wool and experimented with soot mixed with various liquids to make satisfactory face black. For music we used mouth organs, tambourines and jews' harps. Those without instruments sang. We played any songs we knew, as well as carols, and did not think of our guising as having any religious significance. Probably the custom was descended from rituals of pre-Christian times.

We would make our way from house to house, walking behind the white frosted dykes to shelter from the biting winds, the only sound the crackling of ice as our feet broke through the frozen puddles. Joseph Noble used to carry a black metal candle lamp, a tiny gleam in the dark.

As we approached a house, a dog would bark furiously and leap to the limit of its chain, wild with excitement. The door open, we would stand in the pool of light until invited in, our weird appearance causing shrieks of laughter. After our little performance of music and song and a dance that consisted of hopping alternate feet and flapping our elbows like wings, we received a glass of wine, a piece of Christmas cake and a hunk of cheese. Usually the wine was home-made rhubarb or gooseberry, or sometimes non-alcoholic ginger and more rarely a glass of sherry. Each farmhouse kitchen with its huge fire, oil lamp, bright clippy mats and Christmas decorations seemed a haven of comfort contrasted with the raw cold outside.

We became bloated with cake and cheese and began putting it in our pockets where it became a soggy lump. After a few glasses of wine we became tipsy, performed with great gusto and kissed the girls. Gradually, after several visits, the wine took greater effect and we wobbled with legs that seemed made of straw like a scarecrow. We would throw sops of cake to the dogs as we passed and set off for home, giggling, singing snatches of song and stumbling over the styles.

Guising continued if the weather allowed until New Year. If the roads were clear of snow on New Year's Eve we would go to Allendale Town to watch the Fire Festival. We travelled on bikes, or more rarely on the little bus that ran from Allenheads to Allendale especially for this occasion.

The long line of guisers each bearing a blazing tar barrel on his head walked in procession towards the enormous heap of wood prepared in the town square. They threw the barrels at the foot of the heap which immediately ignited and sent flames and smoke skyward. The guisers, in their weird costume, looked like demons in the reflected light of the leaping flames. The town band played *Cock of the North* and, on the stroke of midnight from the nearby church, everyone joined hands to sing *Auld Lang Syne*. The pubs had an extended licence for the evening and there was a great deal of kissing, shouting, singing and dancing in the Square. Groups of people went off first-footing and would drink toasts, laugh and joke throughout most of the night.

We lads would set off homeward on our bikes. One New Year's Eve we saw a wonderful sight; there had been rain earlier and an instant frost had turned each raindrop into a glittering piece of ice; all the trees sparkled like a magic grove.

'Come on, Tom lad. We'll have this dance.' Helen grabbed my

hand, hauled me to my feet, and putting her arm about my waist, began to teach me to waltz. 'One-two-three, one-two-three, on th' toes, keep th' head up lad, la la la!' I seemed to have too many feet. She held me tightly and slowly I began to feel the rhythm.

Helen was a big girl, bright eyed and bonny with frizzy blonde hair. She was a year or two older than me. I could smell the fragrance of her hair and various other exciting odours. 'Friday night is Amami Night', 'Tokalon Face Powder', 'Did you McLean Your Teeth Today?', 'Palmolive Soap, Now I've a Schoolgirl Complexion All Over'. I could feel her warm softness against me.

The fiddler and concertina, accompanied by piano and drums, began a medley of waltz tunes and Helen sang snatches and la la'd in my ear; *That's Peggy O'Neill, My Bonny Lies Over the Ocean, Won't You Buy My Pretty Flowers?, I'm Forever Blowing Bubbles.*

The dance ended and I felt a glow of delight and accomplishment. Helen held my hand when the dance ended. 'Now you must take me back to my seat and say thank you.' She gave me a kiss on the cheek before she sat down.

The dances in Beaumont Hall began with the MC scattering Co-op soap flakes on the floor. Then there would be a Bradford Barn Dance or a Paul Jones to get the evening going. The first dance would be punctuated with bouts of sneezing as the soap flakes circulated.

The first dance provided a variety of sensations; you might be clasped to the bosom of a powerfully-built girl as if for a bout of wrestling and whirled round like a top, or held at arms' length by some fastidious female who would lay a hand on your shoulder to discourage familiarity. One girl always danced with her chin placed on the back of her hand resting on her partner's shoulder as if looking over a wall. We all joined in singing the popular tunes: 'There ain't no sense sitting on the fence all by yourself in the moonlight', 'There's a good time coming be it ever so far away',

'Have you ever been lonely, have you ever been blue?'

We lads began attending dances when we were about fifteen or sixteen, or in my own case when I had acquired some presentable clothes. When I started work at Sipton, Mother bought me a suit from Graves of Sheffield's catalogue – a navy blue suit with a double-breasted waistcoat paid for at half-a-crown per week.

We learned to dance with the help of good-natured girls like Helen, and, by stumbling round with the unfortunate partner until we got the feel of the rhythm and could co-ordinate our movements. None of the dance crazes of the twenties such as the Charleston penetrated the Dales; people were still enjoying the traditional dances.

Helen had told me that when you can waltz, you could do all the dances and I found this mainly true – La Rosa, the St Bernard Waltz, the Waltz Quadrille, Veleta, Pride of Erin, the Spanish Waltz were all variations of the waltz.

We young lads enjoyed the Lancers most of all. As soon as the MC announced the Lancers, there was an immediate buzz of excitement; lads dashed over the floor to grab favourite partners, old folk sought seats at the ends of the hall to be out of harm's way and the MC checked that all sets were complete; if not he would raise an arm and shout for one or two more couples to come onto the floor. Teasdale, the fiddler, would drape his jacket over the back of his chair, and hitch up the sleeves of his shirt under his wire armbands. The Lancers was standing up work. He would play a few introductory bars and the dancers honoured their partners with a quick bow then the dance began. The speed of the playing increased and more excitement was generated as the dance progressed.

The Lancers reached its climax with the big set of four couples; we locked sweaty hands, with the lads on either side of the girls, leant backwards with one foot forward and the other behind to push against the floor. Teasdale played ever faster, the floor sagged and rebounded, we gave shouts and whoops of glee, the girls screamed as they lost their footing and flew out parallel to the floor. The set became a whirligig of brightly coloured dresses, gaudy knickers and pale thighs. The band played a waltz for us to wind down. We gulped in the air thick with perfumes and cigarette smoke as we danced and were pleased to flop into chairs for a rest.

The dance over, we set off in groups or pairs to walk home. The night air was filled with the sound of giggles, laughter, shouts of 'Goodnight' and fragments of conversation; motorbikes were kick-started into life and their headlights stabbed the dark. Girls swung legs over the pillion seats and the bikes roared away leaving the echo and the smell of the exhausts and soon all was quiet again.

For most of us, dancing provided the only social diversion. All age groups attended the dances; those too old to dance enjoyed talking to their friends and listening to the music. Occasionally, a band was hired from Consett. This band, called The Syncopated Five, wore dinner jackets and were considered very posh. The musicians doubled up on various instruments and I saw a piano accordion, a saxophone and a one-stringed Japanese fiddle for the first time. We were overawed by their appearance and professionalism, but in one aspect thought them inferior; the music for the Lancers, as they played it, was very sedate and had none of the zest of Teasdale's rendition.

A Trip to Hexham

Bill had a new pushbike – a racing model with dropped handlebars, caliper brakes and thin red tyres. My old bike that I had bought for half-a-crown was finished so Bill proposed that we should go to the pictures in Hexham sharing his bike. He outlined his plan; we would take it in turns to ride to an agreed spot and then walk on leaving the bike against a dyke. Where there were telegraph poles we would count so many before dismounting, and at the top of steep hills we would both ride with me sitting astride Bill's back. Going up steep hills we would walk together.

We made a detour by Allendale railway station to buy a penny packet of Crayol cigarettes from the machine on the platform. The packet contained two cigarettes which we smoked when we rested at the top of the hill at Catton Beacon.

Most of the way into Hexham was downhill with some long, steep hills where we could swish down with our heads low. We never gave a thought to the fact that most of the way home would be uphill.

In Hexham a woman allowed Bill to leave his bike in her backyard until we needed it. We looked at the entrance to Queen's Hall Cinema and I found, with great glee, that the main feature was a Buster Keaton comedy. We gazed at the stills, filled with anticipation.

To fill in time we strolled about looking in shop windows. Near the Market Place stood a stationer's shop with a display of comic postcards in the window. I think we had never seen a comic postcard before and we dissolved with laughter at the pictures of skinny hen-pecked men with enormously fat wives, innocent curates, naive honeymoon couples, dragon-like landladies, red-nosed drunks and Scotsmen with knobbly knees. We laughed so much at the postcards that the woman behind the counter inside laughed at us. Bill's laughter was highly infectious.

In a bookshop window we saw a special exhibition of Everyman Books. I thought the design on the dust covers looked like a helmet. We gazed with longing at this horde of riches, our foreheads pressed against the glass and twisting sideways to read the titles.

Bill had never been to a picture house before and I had not visited one since I had left Sheriff Hill about four years previously. The sad face of Buster Keaton haunted my memory. Long after I had forgotten every detail of the story, his face would appear in my mind's eye as if I had known him well.

Our journey home was arduous, almost all walking. We toiled up the hills leaning on the bike, one each side of it, and set ourselves targets before we stopped to rest. The occasional downhill ride provided a brief respite. We had nothing to eat and drank water from stone troughs at the roadside.

As we had done when we were schoolboys we discussed the future, but our plans had now changed; we no longer thought of pearl diving on the shores of South Sea Islands or gold digging in Australia or lumberjacking in Canada; we decided we must find a way to get out into the world and made up our minds to join the Royal Navy. We indulged in the imagined delights of visits to picture houses, variety halls and dances in strange towns and meeting beautiful girls.

'We'll buy a Morgan three-wheeler,' Bill said. 'We'll come home on leave in it.'

I was rather astounded by this audacious idea.

'We'll get a second-hand one cheap and do it up.'

Here we were sharing one pushbike between us and Bill was thinking of buying a motor car.

'When we're in the Navy we won't have to pay any lodgings and we'll be able to save up to buy it between us.' He made it sound very feasible.

'Where'll we keep it when we're away at sea?'

We discussed this plan in detail as we trudged up the hills. The future seemed full of unlimited possibilities for romance and adventure.

Working with Men

For most of the year after I left school I was able to get only casual work. The first job was snow clearing, or snow cutting we called it.

'Now lad, I'll show th' how to grease a shovel. Th' must have it ready for when the snow comes. I'll take th' with me and th'll get seven bob a day. Let's have the shovel and a candle end.' I watched Joe Noble hold the shovel over the fire and rub the blade with the candle end. Then he stood it in the corner to cool. 'Now she's ready, lad. We'll get some snow soon, I reckon.' The job done, he sat in a chair by the fire and began to cut twist tobacco from the Oxo tin he used as a baccy box, to fill his pipe.

I looked forward eagerly to a heavy fall of snow and to earning some money; seven shillings a day seemed a fortune to me. When the snow did arrive we nearly slept in; during the night a freakish wind had blown a curved drift of snow like a frozen wave up to the eaves of our cottage and blocked out all daylight. We hurried downstairs and, while I raked out the ashes to prepare a fire, Mother lit the primus stove to make the tea and prepare breakfast. The click-click of the stove pump rang out in the silent world; the wind had dropped and even the hens had stayed in the henhouse and were not grumbling for their breakfast corn as they usually did in early morning. We might have been the only people in the world.

I had to throw out my shovel and jump out of the bedroom window to clear the door and dig a path to the coalhouse. Mother put my lunch into a little haversack; a sausage pie on a saucer, some bacon sandwiches, a piece of gingerbread and a bottle of tea. I wore the puttees Joe Burton had given me, a balaclava helmet and mittens Mother had knitted for me and an old

raincoat. As Joe had advised, I put a handful of hay into each clog to keep my feet warm.

I set off for Joe's farm, worried in case I was late and he had set off without me, but when I arrived he was sitting by the fire, smoking his after breakfast pipe, and seemed in no hurry to get started. 'I think we'll have another cup of coffee before we go, Mary,' he said. Mary prepared two cups from the bottle of Camp coffee. 'We'll mebbies meet up with some of the others along the Lonnen,' Joe said. 'Depends on what the drifts are like.'

We began digging our way along Swinhope Lonnen. The wind had blown some stretches of road clear of snow and created high drifts in others; Joe showed me how to cut out cubes of snow and warned me not to take too big a bite with the shovel or I would tire before the day was done. The work kept us warm.

By mid-day I was very hungry. We built an L-shaped wall of snow cubes as a shelter and stuck our shovels in the snow to sit on. Food had a very special taste in these circumstances; even the cold tea tasted good. After Joe had smoked a pipe of his twist tobacco, we began work again and later met some men cutting snow on the back Lonnen.

Mother had prepared one of my favourite dinners for me: chops cooked in the oven with barley and onion gravy topped with suet dumplings. We drew the table near the fire and I felt the glow of warmth returning to my feet and legs as I ate. Mother draped my outer clothing over a clotheshorse to dry. When I went to bed I was too tired even to remove the oven shelves Mother had put in the bed to warm it and I slept on top of them all night. It seemed I had just lain down when I heard Mother shouting up the stairs for me to come down to breakfast. I was not quite so enthusiastic as on my first day and my body ached.

For a few days we worked clearing the Back Lonnen and other by-roads. We worked in pairs, setting in about twenty yards ahead of the foremost pair and then cutting towards the space where two others coming up from the rear had cut in. We must have looked like the remnants of a defeated army; some men wearing greatcoats from the last war and caps on top of balaclavas, some with puttees, some with leggings, while others wore huggers – old stockings tied round the instep to prevent snow getting into their clogs. Sacks pushed in at the corner and placed over the head and shoulders gave them a monkish appearance.

When the weather was not too bad, most of the men enjoyed the work; it provided a get together for those who rarely saw each other and there was a great deal of banter and brief stops to chat as they passed friends.

On Whetstone Mee, where the road made its way round the side of Killhope towards West Allen and Nenthead, the snowdrifts were so deep we had to work double banked – a couple of men stood half way up the drift and threw out the cubes of snow passed up to them by the couple below. Ahead, the men cutting the lower part of the drift were out of sight and all we could see were the cubes of snow flying up to their mates above them.

This was calm, windless day at first; fragments of

conversations, the sound of occasional laughter and the ringing and scraping noises of shovels on the bare road came clearly through the still air.

The sun came out for a while and it seemed we were on holiday. Some of the ex-soldiers began singing their wartime songs: 'When this bloody war is over, oh how happy I shall be', 'Have you seen the sergeant major? We know where he is, he's hanging on the old barbed wire', 'Take me back to dear old Blighty', 'I love my wife, I love her dearly'.

One day we experienced the coldest and most miserable weather of all, what Dalesmen call a 'cold fresh' when it turns much colder and yet the snow begins to melt – the damp penetrates right through and feet become numb. At bait-time we sought refuge in Robson's byre; his farm stood near the road and was the last farm before the bare moorland. We sat with our backs against the walls, sharing the warmth and comfort with the patient beasts munching hay. They turned their heads from time to time to regard us curiously as they chewed. Mr Robson brought us a kettle of hot tea and some enamel mugs. We drank, cuddling the mugs with our numbed hands and then reluctantly had to pass on the empty mug to be refilled for someone else.

Later in the afternoon a strong west wind blew up, fresh snow was whipped into a blizzard and we could not see more that a few feet ahead. The foreman told us all to disperse and we set off for home, holding our shovels with a corner of the blade resting on a windward shoulder to provide a little shelter. Joe Noble and I stumbled back home to Swinhope, losing our way several times until Joe recognised landmarks and put us on the right track again.

I enjoyed my snow cutting days very much, partly because working with men made me feel grown up. I also looked forward to the paycheck and I was very sorry when all the roads were open.

Another outdoor job that came my way later in the year was to work for a local gamekeeper.

I gazed with curiosity at the gentry assembled on the fell for grouse shooting and listened with wonder to their voices that, my pal Bill said, sounded as if they spoke with a mouthful of hot tatties. I had never before seen or heard a member of the upper classes and I thought their speech sounded almost like a foreign language, I admired their clothes – gaudy tweed jackets, whipcord riding breeches, brightly coloured shirts and tweed hats with feathers stuck in the band. One man, addressed by the others as Sir John, was a real dandy, wearing green corduroy knickerbockers, wool stockings to match, a multicoloured hacking jacket and a silk cravat with a fox head pin on it. He reminded me of Sir Percy Blakeney in *The Scarlet Pimpernel*. I wondered if Richard Hannay and other characters from John Buchan's novels were like these people and spoke as they did.

This was my first day as a beater – driving, the local people called it. After being positioned by the gamekeepers the beaters' job was to spread out in a line and advance towards the butts to drive the grouse to the guns. We would see the grouse falling ahead of us as the guns blazed away – a zooming flight when we disturbed them from their cover and then a quick fall to earth. Occasionally a snipe would arise from a boggy place, fly zigzag for a moment to avoid the guns, and disappear into the distance. I was always delighted that snipe usually escaped. I felt it was wrong to shoot a wild bird.

When the weather was fine I enjoyed beating as it appealed to my love of wild and unspoilt places – the long walks over pollen-laden heather and the ling that sent up clouds of dust at each step, splashing through boggy patches, slithering down bracken-clad slopes by the sides of little burns, scrambling among outcrops of gritstone.

I had never imagined such vast quantities of food as were supplied for the beaters at lunch time – huge joints of roast meat, enormous lumps of butter, stacks of loaves, kegs of beer and stone grey-hens of cider. We sat outside to enjoy our meal while the shooters dined inside a wooden hut. Estate men brought the food in a cart, which later took away the dead grouse. We ate ravenously and the cider made us slightly tipsy. Bill and I tried to mimic the gentry and collapsed with laughter at the ludicrous sounds we uttered.

In a butt we found a pipe left behind by one of the shooters. We later bought an ounce of Afrikaners tobacco and took it in turns to smoke.

Shortly after the grouse shooting season was over, a friend named Robert Spark spoke to the manager at Sipton Lead Mine on my behalf and I was given a job in the washing. On our first day at bait time (as the dinner break was called) we new boys had to face an initiation ceremony. Maurice Liddle, Joseph Noble and I were new boys together and rumours of what we had to face made us apprehensive. We each had to sing a song and be daubed with black axle grease.

We ate our bait in a large room under the office where we clocked in each morning. A huge fire of scrap timber blazed at one end, and wooden benches lined the other three walls. Near the fire stood a table on which we placed our tea cans each morning ready for Tom Hewitson to brew the tea a few minutes before the twelve-o'clock buzzer.

I stood in the middle of the room and sang *All by Yourself in the Moonlight*. I had an audience of about thirty men who stamped their feet on the floor and applauded my feeble effort. After the songs we received our ritual daubing and became members of the Brotherhood of Lead Miners.

The corrugated iron building called 'the washing' was cold, draughty and damp; snow and rain blew in between the overlaps of iron. There was no heating. When the tubs of sludgy lead ore arrived at the surface, they were pushed along a tramway and tipped into a hopper that fed onto a conveyor belt in the washing. My friend Alec McVay, who was about my age, kept the flow of ore going with a tool like an elongated garden hoe. Joseph and I stood beside the conveyor belt picking off the pieces of ore, which were almost pure lead known as 'Potters ore', and putting them in a barrow. When the barrow was full we wheeled it to a shed for cleaning.

A few yards beyond us, the ore dropped into a crushing machine with great iron jaws and jagged teeth that crushed and ground it into particles. The particles dropped into the jigger where a flow of water separated lead from stone. Eventually the lead was loaded into skips and carried by an aerial flight to a dumping place near the roadside for collection by the steam wagon.

I hated the crushing machine with its incessant gashing teeth

and the horrible noise it produced. I was pleased when a piece of scrap iron got into the jaws and choked it to a standstill. I always pretended not to notice a piece of iron going by. We would hear Tommy Dickinson, the foreman, shouting and swearing below us, the fitters would come up to put things right and we would seize the chance to dry our hands and have a quick smoke. Tommy never blamed us for not removing the pieces of iron from the belt. It dawned on me that perhaps the fuss Tommy made was an act put on for the benefit of the manager.

I had been working less than a year at Sipton when it closed down. Though the job had been dreary, uninteresting and badly paid, it was at least regular employment. As a boy of sixteen I received twelve shillings and sixpence per week unemployment benefit.

I was unhappy at this time. I was bitterly shamed of my poverty and becoming increasingly aware of my lack of education. The future looked bleak.

Primrose Time

On fine Sunday evenings during late spring and early summer, youths and girls strolled up and down the road, the girls in groups of two or three linking arms, the lads following behind. Some of the girls went to Chapel and joined the walkers afterwards, but very few young people attended Chapel regularly.

We would gather little bunches of primroses and fasten them behind the press-studs of our caps and parade up and down the road attempting to make contact with the girls in some way, usually by engaging in silly joking and teasing. Sometimes the girls did the teasing and one would snatch a cap which would be thrown from one to another as the owner tried to grab it back. We always wore a handkerchief peeping from the top pocket of our jackets. We were anxious to show off in some way, yet dreading a rebuff or ridicule. I knew laughter was a way through the barrier so I tried feeble jokes and risqué riddles. The trouble was, we had nothing to boast about, nothing with which to show off, nothing to use to impress them or arouse interest. We were peacocks without dazzling tails.

We dressed in our Sunday best – the girls in their bright dresses and coats, the lads in navy blue suits with double breasted waistcoats, wide trousers creased under the mattress, starched white collars, jazzy ties and tweed caps. Some lads wore black and white checked caps obtained by collecting packets from Club cigarettes which were twopence for five, like Woodbines.

A pairing-off game was played according to rules understood by everyone but never expressed; the object was to separate a girl from her friends and persuade her to go for a walk or allow you to walk her home. Every move had to be made obliquely; if you made

a clumsy move you might get a clout over the head with a handbag or a swipe with an open hand to the great merriment of the others. Occasionally a girl would take the initiative by snatching a cap and instead of throwing it to her pals, would run past the others, so allowing herself to be caught by the owner. The pair would walk off snuggling close, the lad's arm round the girl's waist. Being sixteen, I was beginning to feel grown up. Secretly I admired one or two of the girls, but had made no overtures.

Elsie was a dark-haired girl of medium height with refined features and bright eyes that glinted with humour. She was wearing a blue dress and a tweed coat with an imitation fur collar. She walked well, with head held high, and had an air of being superior. We had attended the same school but I did not know her very well as I had not noticed her much at school and she had left about a year before I did. Her mother and father were staunch Chapel folk and I had seen her occasionally at Harvest Festivals and Anniversary Services, but very rarely at other times. Some lads had gone off with her pals and she was left to me.

'Come on then, be matey,' she said, and put her arm through

mine. I was overwhelmed. It was like the dish running away with the spoon. As we walked along I searched in my mind for something to say. She asked me what I was going to do now that Sipton Mine had closed, and told me she wanted to get away from the Dale and farm work. We took a path that led over the fells. 'I'll show you where we used to play when we were bairns. We had a hidey hole that no one knew about where we played shops with boody money.'

Not far from the fell track there was a deep ravine with a little burn flowing at the bottom. Ling and bracken grew on the steep sides and in places there were outcrops of millstone and shale. Elsie led me to a place where a natural overhang covered with ling formed a cave in the bankside. When they were young she and her pals had enlarged the cave by building walls of flat stones and heather turfs that had since grown to bind the walls together. They had made a roof with bed ends from a rubbish tip and covered it with heather. Rusty old tins that crumbled when touched, dilapidated frying pans, saucepans and baking tins lay on the floor.

She picked up a piece of broken china with a blue pattern on it and laughed at her memories. 'We used this for boody money to play shops. The plain bits were pennies, the pieces with patterns on were florins and half-crowns. If they had a bit of gilt on them we called them sovereigns. We made pies, loaves of bread and sausages from clay and played here for hours. No one could find us. I once heard Mam searching and yelling 'Elsie', but I never let on. I didn't want anyone to find out about our secret place. I got into trouble when I got back and Dad gave me a twanking on the backside with his slipper.'

'Let's have a spring clean,' she said, beginning to throw out all the old tins and pans. We made a new floor with some russet-coloured bracken and sat down. I was enchanted with her nearness. She wore no make-up except a sweet-scented face cream.

The cave had a damp peaty smell. We could hear the faint sound of the burn below. Over the crest of the opposite bank we could see, in the distance, several farmhouses nestling on the dale side.

'Come on then, give me a kiss,' she said. I tried to tell her how I felt but she put a finger on my mouth and said 'Shush.' I lost all notion of time. The setting sun glinted on the windows of distant farmhouses like heliographed signals.

'I'll have to go,' she said, 'or I'll get into bother at home. You can walk with me as far as the larch tree along our road. Dad will be waiting up and won't go to bed till I'm in. Most likely I'll get a sermon for my supper.' She began to comb her hair and asked me to brush off the telltale pieces of bracken on her coat.

I left her beside the larch tree that looked like a pagoda and stood near the little footpath that branched off towards the house. We kissed goodnight. She said she would meet me on Wednesday, here beside the larch tree. I watched her run down the footpath. She gave a little wave as she went round the corner of the house. I made my way home feeling I could turn cartwheels for joy.

On Wednesday evening I was at the appointed place beside the larch tree about half an hour too soon and waited and waited, but she did not come. I stayed there until it was nearly dark and the lamplight was sending out a pale glow on the flagstones in front of the house but I did not see her. I returned every night but waited in vain.

Mother kept complaining about my behaviour and bad temper at home. 'What on earth is the matter with you lad? You're like a bear with a sore head!'

On the following Sunday evening I went round to the back of the chapel to peep in the window. I could see her with her sisters and parents in a pew near the front; she was wearing the same blue dress.

The sermon was in full swing with the preacher making big gestures to ram home his points. I could hear several members of the congregation shouting out fervently 'Amen!' and 'Praise the Lord!' At last the final hymn, *Shall we Gather at the River,* began. I dashed round to the porch at the front to meet Elsie coming out. She gave me a prim Sunday smile, said 'Hello', and before I could gather my thoughts and frame my questions she moved off with her family. One of her sisters turned her head to look at me and giggled with the back of her gloved hand over her mouth.

For several Sundays afterwards I joined the other strollers hoping that Elsie would be there, but I saw her no more and she was lost to me forever.

Within a couple of years the custom of strolling in primrose time had come to an end. Lads became divided into knights and peasants. A knight of the wheel mounted on his AJS, BSA, Norton or Ariel and armoured with thigh leggings, heavy coat, gauntlets and goggles would swoop down and chat to the admiring girls as he sat astride his gleaming bike.

'Hop on and I'll take th' for a spin,' he'd say to the favoured lady. A brief display of stockings and thigh as the lady swung her leg over the pillion, the bike kicked into life, the lady put her arms around her knight's waist and snuggled her face into his back. The bike took off with a roar leaving a little cloud of fumes, the footrest scraped the road as bike and passenger leaned over at a perilous angle round bends; scarves streamed out behind them like pennants.

We peasants watched wistfully and longed for the day when we might possess a bike of our own. This was the golden age of motor cycling when there were almost no cars or buses on the roads. Sometimes we saw a motorbike leaning against the dyke near some woodland, with no sign of rider or passenger.

The primroses that grew by the roadsides were doomed. New

and improved methods of keeping the roadsides tidy killed them off, and, as times changed, the custom of parading on fine Sunday evenings died out too.

The End of the Hay Ride

Near the side of Blackcleugh Burn stood the remains of an ancient house. Only one of its roof timbers remained, an unhewn tree trunk with part of its thick side branch left on to make up the length required to span the walls. The trunk was half rotted and moss-green but still in position. No roofing flagstones lay round about, so the house had probably been roofed over with turves of heather.

My brother Norman and I spent many hours by the burnside near the old house in that kind of timelessness that young boys sometimes live in. This area had a peculiar fascination for us. We tickled for trout in the little burn, paddled in the deep pools and searched for birds' nests. From further downstream, near the place where the little burn joined the Swinhope burn, we often heard the raucous cry of the corncrake, but we never saw the bird and we looked vainly for its nest among the long grass. The sandpiper's nest was easy to find as we could see the place on a sandy bank where the bird darted out like an arrow. It was a neat little nest with the eggs lying pointed ends towards the centre. Occasionally we saw a heron flying up the Swinhope burn, looking for trout and frogs.

New Milk Spring near where the two burns met, Old Thoomy told us, had medicinal properties and was good for what she called 'belly-wark' (belly ache). We went to this spring to drink, kneeling to cup the water in our hands. It was beautiful water always clear and cool. In this calm, peaceful area we saw no one and heard only the birds' cries, the occasional thrum of a snipe, a dog barking now and then or the skirring sound of a man sharpening a scythe in the distance. We were perfectly happy and left only when driven homewards by hunger.

The old house at Blackcleugh must have been a remnant of the kind of houses the people of Swinhope lived in before the industrial revolution. Between the legendary time when the White Canons from Blanchland Abbey hunted the wild boar in Swinhope and the beginning of the lead mining industry in the eighteenth century nothing much is known. The early settlers named places, enclosed fields with dykes of gritstone, killed off ling, bracken, rushes and scrubland to create meadows and pastures, and built their houses of stone with heather roofs.

They gave the places names that sound like poetry: Thorny Knowe, Pasture Nook, High Hay Rake, Blackcleugh, Elpha Green, New Milk Spring, Rowantree Cleugh. Some of the people's names are preserved in place names: Nan Davidson's Cleugh, Wattie Bell's Cairn, Waggot's Fold, Goodfellow's Sikes, Varty's Fold.

The gritstone dykes look so natural they seem to have grown in their place. They have stood firmly for centuries and follow the contours of the land even when it is almost vertical. The stones called copes, on top of the dykes, are always worked to give a tidy finish. If you look carefully, you can see different styles of craftsmanship; some builders used very long throughstones, the stones going right through the dyke and jutting out on each side to give strength; some builders used short ones, while others used none and left a smooth-sided dyke. The men who built these dykes were remarkable craftsmen. Dyke building must have taken place over a long period of time as people gradually cultivated more moorland by draining and killing off bracken, ling and rushes.

The early dwellers in Swinhope must have been self-sufficient. There was a mill in Swinhope, but they probably bought grain – rye and oats grow in more fertile places. They cut peat and brown coal for fuel. The brown coal called 'crow coal' was mixed with clay to make balls called 'cats'. One of the houses in Swinhope, where the clay was obtained, is named 'Clayhole'. Their sheep would provide them with wool to spin and weave into cloth for garments.

The people of Swinhope escaped history. There are no written records and few local legends. They apparently believed in witches as every house has its Witch Elm or Rowan tree to guard against them and thought that elves played on Elpha Green and lived in limestone caves called the Elf Holes. There was no church and no chapels before the late eighteenth century so perhaps they knew little of Christianity. The White Canons from Blanchland may have travelled there to instruct the people, but there is no record as far as I know of this, and since Blanchland Abbey was dissolved in 1536 there could hardly have been any religious instruction for more than two hundred years until Wesley brought about the religious revival in the Dales in the late eighteenth century.

For centuries the people in these remote areas lived with very little contact with the outside world. They built their own houses, made their own furniture, farmed their land, spun and wove cloth, quarried stone, and conformed to their own code of conduct. It is hardly surprising that the Dalespeople of Northumberland were such a fiercely independent folk.

We lads in Swinhope used to explore the tunnels of the old drift mines bored into the flanks of Killhope. The stonework of the tunnels was as carefully hewn as if for the vaults of a church. We had to walk in a crouching fashion in a space just big enough for a man leaning forward to push a tub of stone or lead ore. Water seeped through from above all the time, dropping at irregular intervals into pools on the floor with resonant plops and making an eerie kind of music. There was a strong smell of wet earth and stone and it was always cool. We would advance slowly by the light of a feeble candle, fearful yet compelled by curiosity. If the candlelight went out we were really scared and stumbled back, longing to see the little point of light at the entrance. I terrified myself by imagining that a roof fall would entomb us forever.

The drifts, the dam which had been constructed to provide water to wash the lead ore, and the high slag heaps were all that remained of a flourishing lead mining industry which had lasted for more than sixty years and provided a period of relative prosperity for the people of Swinhope. The mines stopped work in 1872 and the population declined rapidly. I often wondered if there were any Swinhope people among the strikers who sailed away to settle on the banks of the Illinois in America.

To us lads in Swinhope the isolated region at the foot of Killhope was a wonderful playground: we swam and floated rafts on the dam and made slides on the frozen surface in the winter. We jumped from the tops of the slag heaps landing on our heels on the loose slag to break our fall, launching ourselves outwards as far as possible in order to enjoy the brief moment of free fall before landing.

Nearby grew a veritable forest of bracken where we ate our sandwiches and drank cold tea from a Newcastle Pale Ale bottle and sometimes smoked a Woodbine, enjoying the feeling of seclusion and secrecy boys love so much.

Sometimes we climbed to the top of Killhope and clambered up the cairn from which it was said one could see three counties and Scotland in the far distance. No matter how calm the day there was always a strong wind blowing up there. We would cling to the wooden pole at the top of the cairn with the wind in our faces looking to the mountains of Lakeland, Wordsworth country; but at that time I had never even heard his name.

The tramp we called Rushy Legs appeared in Swinhope each year in early summer time. He had a face like wrinkled leather. He always wore leggings of neatly plaited rushes and an old mackintosh, bleached by the sun and rain to a light straw colour and tied around his waist with a piece of rope. His pockets bulged with mysterious packages and he carried a bundle over his shoulder. Bunches of curly grey hair jutted out behind his greasy cap. He carried a stick and walked with his head down ignoring everyone. When he passed the schoolyard children threw stones at him but he ignored this also. Jack Reed of  Hope Head farm used to allow him to spend the night in his barn after taking the precaution of removing the matches from Rushy's pockets. The tramp knew the houses where he would be given his dinner. He used to eat his meal sitting with his back against the garden wall balancing the plate on his bunched up knees.

No one ever found out exactly where he came from or where he went to after leaving Swinhope. One year he did not arrive and folk remarked on his absence. He came no more.

Peddlers arrived from time to time, carrying dilapidated suitcases tied round with rope and filled with shoelaces, needles, thread, ribbons, pins and safety pins. They were the last of their kind and were not seen again after about 1930.

The gypsies used to camp on a stretch of greensward near the ruins of a house with the peculiar name of Gaping Geese. I would stare with fascination at the gaily-painted caravans with their little chimneys and tiny flights of steps to the door. In fine weather they sat out of doors beside a wood fire on which they cooked. The women went from house to house selling clothes pegs, telling fortunes and begging old clothes while the men tried to buy or sell horses. I always thought they were a happy and carefree people. I envied the boys because they didn't have to go to school and could ride horses and drive a two-wheeled flat cart. I do not think anyone regarded them with dislike or hostility, but were a little wary of them. Like Rushy Legs and the pedlars the gypsies soon disappeared from the area.

'By, what a claister,' Old Thoomy would say referring to the muddy state of the track as she picked her way cat-like down past our cottage at High Swinhope Mill. The nickname Thoomy meant like a thumb. It was very apt as she was short with broad hips. She walked in a waddling way because of some kind of defect in her hip. People said she doddled. I never saw her dressed in any other way than in the old-fashioned black skirt, white pinafore and blouse, clogs with steel buckles and a mob-cap. Mother avoided her because she could not understand her speech. Thoomy spoke rapidly in a high-pitched complaining tone; as Mother said 'like the hens on a cold day waiting for crowdy.' Thoomy used so many strange words and forms of speech that it was very difficult to get more than a vague idea of what she was talking about. Mother would put in an odd yes or no for politeness but often got it wrong.

'Abut nay,' Thoomy would cry and shake her head vigorously when Mother put in a 'yes' when it should have been a 'no'.

'By, but as was jealous,' she said one day, and we couldn't work out why she was jealous. She was using 'jealous' in the old English sense of being suspicious. She used terms such as 'She's well saddered' – serves her right; 'I'se wea for her' – I'm sorry for her; 'Yammering on' – complaining; 'A bowdikite' – a worthless person; 'Dowly' – melancholy. I regret now that I did not listen more carefully to this rich language from the past.

At Easter time Thoomy brought us a present of paste eggs – eggs boiled with onion skins or scraps of coloured cloth to produce pretty patterns on the shells. At Christmas she gave us teacakes shaped like men with currants for eyes and mouth. She called them Yule Doos. The giving of Yule Doos at Christmas was a long forgotten custom and no one knew of their significance.

Some of Thoomy's suggested remedies for various ailments were very strange; she recommended curing a sore throat by gargling with yeddle – cow's urine warmed in a pan; sitting with your feet immersed in a bucket of snow to cure chilblains; a sock filled with hot salt held on an aching ear; poultices made of mouldy bread for boils and sores; spreading honey on burns and scalds and drinking the water of certain springs as a cure for stomach ailments. She had a wide knowledge of the medicinal value of herbs and local plants.

The boys sometimes played tricks on Thoomy. Once they climbed on the roof of her cottage and dropped stones down the chimney. She also had a cure for this; the next time they tried it, she was prepared, when she heard their steps on the roof she threw paraffin oil on the fire and the chimney belched sparks and red-hot soot just as they approached it. The cure worked.

Like the peddlers, the tramps and the gypsies, Old Thoomy was part of a vanished past.

Until the early thirties the greatest change in the lives of the people had been the advent of the lead mining industry and the growth of Methodism following Wesley's religious revival which happened at about the same time. The First World War did not change life in the Dales as much as it had done in other parts of England.

When Wharton's Bus Company began a regular service between Allenheads and Hexham life began to change. Previously people had to take Shield's or Foster's little bus to the railway station at Catton and catch the train. The new bus service made the journey easier, quicker and cheaper and many people who had rarely been further than Allendale Town began to make frequent journeys to shop in Hexham.

This was the age of the bus and the motorbike. Young men began to travel, to visit picture houses and dances, and to marry girls from strange localities. In the old days young men and women had been restricted in their choice of partners to families living nearby, generally within walking distance or at the most a bike ride away.

The crystal wireless set was a kind of toy and very few people bothered with it, but when sets without headphones and with a speaker powered by accumulators were invented, 'listening in' became popular. Everyone said that local speech would soon die out now that people listened so much to formal pronunciation, but fortunately this did not happen completely.

Bill Philipson and I reported to the Royal Navy recruiting office in Rye Hill, Newcastle upon Tyne. A doctor gave us a medical test and a Petty Officer in uniform set us an educational test in English and maths. Afterwards we went into a pub on Westgate Hill and, feeling like swaggering sailors, a pair of hurricane jacks, ordered a glass of rum. The plump middle-aged barmaid in her black bulging dress regarded us with amusement. 'Anything in it? A drop of peppermint?' We declined. Neat rum was our drink. We drank them quickly and spluttered and nearly choked. I thought it had a loathsome taste but pretended to enjoy it. We had another before going to catch our train to Hexham. On the way home we began to giggle, made jokes about the plump barmaid and talked about

the wonderful life ahead. A few days later I received a buff
envelope letting me know I had failed the educational test. Bill
passed the exam and went off to barracks in Portsmouth. I never
saw him again. We were never at home at the same time. He was
killed on the famous HMS *Kelly* in the Mediterranean and his
name is on the War Memorial at Allenheads.

I managed later to get into Gravesend Sea School and had a
few months' training in seamanship, partly in the shore
establishment and partly on an old sailing ship called the *Triton*
moored in the river. Then I was sent with my sea bag and donkey's
breakfast – a pallet of straw for a bed, and two woollen blankets –
to Cardiff to join a tramp steamer called *Atlantic City* as a deck
boy. She was lying by the dockside and was bound for Vancouver
to load grain.

The gangway was not out and a long ladder rested against the
ship's side. She looked enormous. I left my bedding on the
quayside and began to climb up with my sea bag over my shoulder,
holding on to the ladder with
one hand.

'You silly prat!' a man
on deck yelled.

The end of a heaving
line fell on my head. I
looked up and saw a man
standing above me holding a
line.

'Get back down and bend
on your bloody sea bag first!'

I fastened my bag to the
line. My new life had begun.

Afterword – Tom's Story

Tom Bell did not remain long at sea. After a few months, he jumped ship and lived rough on the streets of London before contacting a relative who paid his passage home to the North East by sea on a collier. He was met on his return, penniless and clothed in rags, by his uncle Tom Newton and his cousin Andy.

Some time later he was drafted into, or joined, the Army. This did not suit him either and he deserted his unit, made his way back to Allendale and hid out in The Intake, a vacant smallholding near Allenheads, previously occupied by his mother, Ada, and her new husband, Johnnie Philippson. His cousins recall him living fearfully and secretly in the empty cottage, ankle-deep in eggshells.

He then rejoined the Merchant Navy, now, in wartime, a far more dangerous option than the Army. He served as a deckhand on the Atlantic convoys and was torpedoed twice. He remained in the Merchant Navy for the duration of the war, then married Mildred, a girl from Gateshead, and returned to the dales to live at Sparty Lea.

Eventually, at a mature age, he entered university, took a degree in English and became a schoolteacher. He and his wife had two daughters. He died in 1985 and his wife died in 2006.

His brother, Norman, joined the Royal Marines as a boy bandsman and served until 1954, when he also entered university to take a degree in English and become a teacher. Norman returned to Allenheads and lived there until he died in 1976. Both brothers are buried in Allenheads churchyard.

Of the friends and family mentioned in the text, cousin Tom Newton joined the army, was captured at Dunkirk and spent the war in a prison camp but was tragically killed at the very moment of his liberation when the US Army truck in which he and other released POWs were travelling ran off a precipice.

Bill Philippson, Tom Bell's best friend, and a member of the same well-known local family as his stepfather, Johnnie, joined the Navy in 1936 and was killed in action off Crete in HMS *Kelly*. Joe Noble, the family's neighbour, friend and benefactor, was severely injured by a delayed explosion as he and his neighbours examined a German bomb which had landed on the fellside.

David Brown, 2007